# Of the People,
# By the People,
# For the People

# Of the People,
# By the People,
# For the People

# A National
# K-12
# Service Initiative

Sandy McKane

iUniverse LLC
Bloomington

**Of the People, By the People, For the People**
**A National K-12 Service Initiative**

*iUniverse books may be ordered through booksellers or by contacting:*

*iUniverse LLC*
*1663 Liberty Drive*
*Bloomington, IN 47403*
*www.iuniverse.com*
*1-800-Authors (1-800-288-4677)*

*ISBN: 978-1-4759-6710-4 (sc)*
*ISBN: 978-1-4759-6712-8 (hc)*
*ISBN: 978-1-4759-6711-1 (ebk)*

*Printed in the United States of America*

*iUniverse rev. date: 06/25/2013*

I dedicate this book to the innovative project originators who have brought solutions to areas of need around the world. May this book stimulate a national service initiative that will honor your work with support and widespread replication.

I dedicate this book as well to our children, who seek inclusion and a voice in the way our world works. May we find the humility as adults to embrace the purity of their vision.

# CONTENTS

▼

Foreword.................................................................................... ix

Acknowledgments ..................................................................... xi

Introduction ............................................................................ xiii

Part One: "Of the People"............................................................1

    A Plethora of Outstanding Service Projects.............................1

    Service Learning: The Inclusion of Our Children ..................11

    Food2Share: A Service Learning Project.................................14

Part Two: "By the People" ..........................................................23

    A National K-12 Service Curriculum.....................................23

    K-12 Service Learning Outline................................................25

    Specific Models in Specific Grades ..........................................25

        K-12 Snapshot ...................................................................26

        Kindergarten: Caring for Animals....................................29

        First Grade: Hospital Dolls ..............................................32

        Second Grade: Violence Intervention

            Safe House Gift Bags .............................................36

        Third Grade: Sister City—A Global Service

            Learning Component .....................................................41

        Fourth Grade: Disabilities Awareness ...............................51

        Fifth Grade: Food2Share....................................................62

        Sixth Grade: Recycling and Zero Waste............................64

        Grades Seven through Twelve....................................................73

        A K-12 Service Learning Journal............................................77

Part Three: "For the People" ......................................................78

    Sustainability.............................................................................78

    Schools at the Center of Our Communities.............................81

    National and Community Checklists.......................................84

One Central Office......................................................................85

The Logic of Starting Young.............................................87

A Common Heritage of Civic Engagement.....................89

Moving Forward.................................................................91

The Quest to Realize the K-12 Service Initiative...........92

An Addendum .........................................................................97

# FOREWORD

by New York State Senator James L. Seward

▼

The poet Audre Lorde once said, "There are no new ideas. There are only new ways of making them felt." The work that Sandy McKane has devoutly prepared embodies that sentiment—though I would say she has come as close as anyone to conceiving a completely new concept.

Sandy has succeeded in exploring a broad spectrum of work developed by great thinkers and weaving the threads together into an artful tapestry that can be utilized to wholly modify our educational system.

The world is evolving at a rapid pace, and our schools must develop and grow in kind for the students of today to rise and take the mantle of future leadership. Instilling children with a true spirit of community service is an avenue that must be pursued to help guide them toward this lofty but essential goal.

One of the most difficult steps in advancing such an ambitious agenda is deciding where to start. The beauty in this instance is that a ready-made network is in place. Utilizing our schools as a jumping-off point for community service not only makes sense but is fairly simple to accomplish.

Schools already fulfill a pivotal role in each and every community, small and large, from east coast to west coast. A feeling of unity and pride emanates from our schools and touches all. Success in the classroom, on the playing field, or on the school stage cannot be quantified through empirical facts and figures, but there is no quarreling with the ideal. Adding pure community service to the equation will build on the influence our schools already have and extend their reach exponentially.

As you read this book, which can best be described as a call to action, you will become an active participant in advancing this concept. No doubt you will visualize ways to put this strategy into practice in your own school. Take the next step and involve a neighboring district—you will strengthen the bonds that already exist and set in motion the K-12 service learning model.

# ACKNOWLEDGMENTS

▼

This book represents the efforts "of the people, by the people, for the people"—the many who have taken us thus far in together creating a model for our children and community members in need. Without these efforts and contributing influences, the ideas presented would not have formed.

To Fran Hollon, for his professional validation of my initial inquiries, and for identifying the "fire in my belly" spirit that pursued a particular perspective on service learning.

To Senator Seward, for his interest, accessibility, unwavering support, and efforts to help move this work forward.

To Steve Pindar, who brought a powerhouse of energy and commitment to help get Food2Share off the ground, and Daphne Ward, for her always-inspired support of the developing model.

To all the teachers, principals, and superintendents, who took steps with me to create the elementary grade, age-appropriate service learning models for this initiative with their students.

To the students, who enthusiastically engaged in projects to better their communities, and who confirmed without prompting the potential of replicating these projects nationwide.

To the staff of community-based organizations, who educated me about a wide variety of services for those in need, who worked with teachers to create projects of significant community value, and who confirmed the logic of widespread replication to support their counterparts nationwide.

To the community members from all walks of life, who offered positive reinforcement for this idea and acknowledging that it makes sense—that we need this for our children, and for our communities.

To my husband, Tim, for his objective and constant support of my interests and abilities beyond the narrow framework of music that others had defined for me early in my life.

To Genevieve, my first child, who brought the purity of expression of the young child into my life and brought invaluable editing and insight to me as I wrote this book.

To Charlotte, for showing me when she was little how capable she was if given opportunity and respect.

# INTRODUCTION

▼

This book tackles a topic most would shy away from: addressing the whole of our local, national, and world challenges through a single organizational structure. To suggest there is a way to actually get a handle on the whole of our communities' needs and problem-solving efforts may seem ludicrous at first. If, however, we consider our numbers and the quantity of outstanding problem-solving models often created by "lay experts," logic might direct our thoughts differently. Add to this mix not only the often-unharnessed energy of our youth but also the desire of children to become engaged in their world, and we can begin to see some rather large areas of untapped resources.

Consider further our schools with the mission and personnel to prepare students for citizenship—to graduate young adults who have the academic skills and knowledge to problem solve in a variety of real-world contexts at home and beyond. College professors and students build on this foundation by pursuing in-depth studies in many topic areas, including community and environmental problem solving.

We have means of communication that can unite us in a heartbeat to share not only models and solutions but also to inspire outcomes easily tracked into cumulative data that could shift our focus from the magnitude of needs to the magnitude of solutions. We could map out and address our challenges with schools at the center of the process, placing our children and young adults—the next generation—at the center of operations.

We have all the pieces necessary to organize ourselves:

- Community-based organizations that identify needs
- Outstanding project models
- Schools dedicated to educating and preparing children for the adult world
- Service learning that connects classrooms with solving genuine human and environmental problems

- Parents, grandparents, aunts, uncles, church members, service organization members, and others who care about creating a better world for all of us
- The Internet for communication
- Our intellectual abilities to problem solve, assess, and organize

This book is for everyone who cares about the environment, for everyone who believes in service to others, and for everyone who shares the hope that there is a way to unite with others to meet the challenges we face.

We can create a unified whole of operations in which we work together efficiently and comprehensively toward the overall goal of world health and stability. I do not hold a terminal degree that qualifies me to make this assertion; I don't even know one exists. I simply see a solution that has prompted me to leave my professional area of work to nurture this idea because I am inspired by it and, perhaps most important, because I am an American.

# PART ONE

▼

# "Of the People"

We have generated a wealth of solutions—project resources—among ourselves. We have created a vehicle for connecting service and learning in our schools: service learning. We have demonstrated humanitarian outreach to others and concern for the environment.

## A PLETHORA OF OUTSTANDING SERVICE PROJECTS

Outstanding service projects that address specific and critical human and environmental needs develop at home and abroad. Somewhere within humanity is the ability to care for others, even those we will never know in countries we will never visit. We even find it in our hearts to care for endangered animals that we would never invite into our homes. Our outreach, which begins as ideas and converts to action, is a powerful force.

Who among us has not heard of a wonderful and needed service project? Perhaps someone we know has created such a project. I supported my daughter, Charlotte, in creating a project in our community. Between the ages of five and eighteen she raised and managed over $70,000 for community-based organizations, creating monthly reports throughout this time for her supporters to share how the funds were spent (charlottescircle. com). She was capable of contributing and was happy to engage in the adult world. Her project touched on the power of the individual sustained commitment, prompting further questions and exploration.

Several years into Charlotte's project, the director of our United Way office brought the issue of food insecurity in our community to my attention, as periodic canned food drives weren't enough. When I searched online for other food-garnering models that support food banks, I found one in Florida (inspired by a project in Kentucky), one in Kansas, and one in Georgia. These project models provided enough ideas for us to create an initiative in our community in New York. The term "United States" took on a new meaning in this context as ideas from many states converged in the model we created.

The needs in our community existed in others. We were not alone in facing this challenge, and we could access solutions created by others elsewhere. Americans were doing what they do best—solve problems in existing systems or create new systems. Our unity was palpable.

I collected descriptions of projects that made a difference or created a solution—even part of a solution—for an area of human or environmental need. I started organizing them by topic and contacting project originators, in some cases creating replications with project originators and managers.

One question people ask when coming together to problem solve is, "How are others addressing this need?" Mayors and governors, members of various committees, and others meet to discuss similar challenges and seek solutions others may have already found. On the other end of the spectrum, project originators often seek replication of their work nationwide, knowing that the challenges they have successfully tackled exist elsewhere.

As I continued to organize projects and topic areas in a database, I saw it as a checklist of projects that could be available in all communities. A national checklist of projects would provide solutions that others could replicate. It would even bring community needs—of which we might be unaware—to our attention, along with solution-bearing project models. Such a collection of projects would inspire us as they touch upon our demonstrated ability, our ingenuity, and our commitment to models of solution. They would be "of the people."

# National Projects Checklist

## Food

> ➤ Non-perishable food collections
> ➤ Perishable food collection from farms, grocery stores, food service, restaurants, hunters
> ➤ Mobile meals
> ➤ Weekend food backpacks for students
> ➤ Summer lunches for youth
> ➤ Nutrition and cooking education
> ➤ Community gardens
> ➤ Pay-what-you-can restaurants

## Outreach

> ➤ Hospital patients
> ➤ Nursing home residents
> ➤ The elderly
> ➤ People with disabilities
> ➤ Teen moms
> ➤ Native Americans
> ➤ Military: active-duty personnel, families, veterans

## Shelters, Safe Houses

> ➤ Personal hygiene and cleaning items
> ➤ Clothing: for winter, for work, pajamas, socks
> ➤ Rehabilitation, job training, employment
> ➤ Alternative housing, apartment sharing, affordable rentals
> ➤ Disasters: preparedness, relief, cleanup, rebuilding

## Safety

> ➤ Assessment, networking
> ➤ Defusing gangs, mentoring youth
> ➤ Prisons: re-entry programs, job training, therapeutic activities

## Environment

> ➤ Recycling
> ➤ Alternative energy
> ➤ Wildlife
> ➤ Nature

*As new projects are developed or additional needs are identified,*
*the National Projects checklist will naturally expand.*

# The Depth of Our Problem Solving

I would read about a single service project and be inspired by the work taking place. This inspiration heightened as I gathered projects under specific topics. The quantity of solution making and the variety of approaches became apparent, and solutions seemed more plausible with this information in mind. To share this perspective, I have chosen a single topic to highlight the depth of problem solving among ourselves.

## Mentoring Our Youth: Filling the Void

Many adults are mentoring our youth, often restructuring their professional lives to focus exclusively on caring for the welfare of our youth. Commitment, creativity, and flexibility are the typical markings of these mentors. They find the greatest satisfaction in transforming negatives into positives. They often work long hours with little or no pay to achieve the ultimate reward—the rejuvenation of positive life direction in youth.

In the topic of mentoring our youth, the most intense challenge is in situations where gangs have taken over neighborhoods, resulting in violence and instability. Gang leaders know our youth seek inclusion and a sense of family, of belonging; of even more value, our youth have time and energy that can be redirected.

None of us—regardless of where we live—can afford to ignore the extreme outcomes of gang culture. Shades of gang mentality pop up in bullying and cliques, and terrorist organizations work with great similarity to gangs, wielding a wide sphere of influence. Such an infection requires an antidote that will secure health in all our communities.

The solution builders who address the severe stages of this societal illness in the urban trenches can help guide us toward an antidote. Their work suggests ways to strengthen the educational foundation on which youth can build lives positively integrated with their communities.

Service models that mentor where gangs are active are replacing and restoring the growth potential of youth already caught in the web of gangs. These models educate to prevent gang involvement and provide alternatives for youth. The models below come from Illinois, Massachusetts, New York, Rhode Island, and Washington, D.C. Commonalities and distinctions exist in these youth mentoring projects created by ourselves as Americans.

## Council for Unity—Bob De Sena, Brooklyn, NY, 1975

Youth are empowered to develop nonviolent solutions to violence and bias in their environments. Gang members are gathered to talk and take the lead in finding solutions without violence. The organization works with schools, businesses, youth organizations, law enforcement, and correctional facilities. Safety, unity, and achievement are mission goals that inform curricular programs, training, and interventions. The overwhelming majority of students who participate in their curricular programs go on to college.

## Guardian Angels—Curtis Sliwa, NYC, NY, 1979

Inner-city youth are encouraged to take responsibility in cleaning and safeguarding their neighborhoods by patrolling streets, subways, and events. CyberAngels, created in 1995, extends protection to Internet threats, which are difficult to detect.

## Boston Ten Point Coalition—Boston, MA, 1992

This ecumenical group of Christian clergy and lay leaders focus on providing a nurturing environment for high-risk youth who manifest violent, callous, or self-destructive behaviors; youth whom other agencies are frequently unable to serve.

## Ceasefire—Chicago, IL, 2000

Ceasefire detects and interrupts the spread of violent behavior, using well-trained individuals who have credibility in their communities. These professionals know who has influence, who to talk to, and how to anticipate and de-escalate violent situations. As outreach workers, "interrupters," and canvassers, they work to resolve conflicts through intervention and mediation and connect those beyond the reach of traditional social systems with resources. CeaseFire takes a public-health approach to public safety in that it views violence as a disease from which we can recover.

## Institute for the Study and Practice of Nonviolence—Teny Gross, Providence, RI, 2001

This organization hires ex-offenders to speak from their own experiences and convince young people not to answer the loss of their friends with more shootings and bloodshed. These ex-offenders, trained in violence intervention, work in close partnership with Providence police.

### First Response Ministry—Greater Love Tabernacle Church (GLT) Michael Person, William Dickerson, Dorchester, MA, 2001

When a homicide occurs, GLT rushes to the scene to offer support to homicide victims' families and tough love to those who witnessed or participated in a crime. They work to diffuse tension, plan for funerals, help witnesses come forward, and encourage perpetrators to turn themselves in, emphasizing accountability and preventative education for those not yet caught in the cycle of violence.

### Mentoring Today—Whitney Louchheim and Penelope Spain, Washington, D.C., 2005

Boys under age eighteen get help with legal issues, housing, and family relationships before and after their release from jail to ensure successful reintegration into their families and communities. Mentoring Today makes connections with youth four months before their scheduled releases and continues beyond as needed.

### Youth Services—Cook County, Chicago, IL 1995

Pretrial and post trial youths not considered dangerous (after a complex screening process) receive alternatives to jail that include home confinement (leaving home only for school), an electronic bracelet monitoring system, and a reporting-center program. Instead of being jailed and stigmatized, these youth can live at home and go to school while spending five hours each evening at a center that provides transportation, a meal, and programming that ranges from current-events discussions and bowling to pet therapy and victim-impact panels. This effort reduces the population in detention; the majority of youth get to court on time and crime-free.

### Teen Courts—Over 1,200 teen courts in 49 states

Youth and adult volunteers help with the disposition and sentencing of juveniles and delinquents referred to local youth and teen courts. These courts hold juveniles accountable for their delinquent and criminal behaviors, promote restorative justice principles, and help educate youth about the legal system, incorporating civic and service life lessons.

## ROCA—Mary Baldwin, Chelsea, MA, 1988

This program helps young people ages fourteen to twenty-four from a variety of troubled circumstances reengage in society through education, employment, and life-skills programming. They are visited at home, taken to and from school, and provided with a safe environment that includes free dinners, a gym, music labs, and training in cabinetmaking, carpentry, jewelry making, dance, nutrition, and cooking.

While these projects reflect mentoring prompted by the presence of gangs and criminal activity, the projects below embody a transition toward mentoring youth with activities to "fill the void" that otherwise could be filled with destructive vices.

Our youth become vulnerable to destructive choices when there is vacant space, when they have not discovered constructive areas of interest to fill out the larger dimension of their lives. Our schools are not enough, and programs for music, theater, and sports are not available nationwide for all youth. These programs as well do not offer sufficient variety or sustained engagement for all our youth. Just like adults, the scope of interest and gift among our youth is highly varied.

Typically, the project topics that follow are based on the personal backgrounds or interests of the projects' originators. They may come from the perspective of a remedy, a preventative alternative, or simply the desire to share and engage with youth. The projects provide an opportunity for youth to learn and grow and a safe place where they feel dignity and care for their person—a family context. Providing our youth with activities and inclusion with us builds community and protection against negative influences for us all.

The models below come from California, Florida, Massachusetts, Maryland, Missouri, New Jersey, New York, Oregon, Pennsylvania, and Texas.

## Tia Chucha's Centro Cultural and Bookstore—Luis Rodriguez, Sylmar, CA, 2001

This bookstore has a performance hall and an art and music studio where writers share their work at open mikes and youth can record demo tapes or poetry. Youth are encouraged to replace graffiti with mural painting and learn about Native American rituals as spiritual outlets. It is the only bookstore in the nation's second-largest Mexican community and also serves as a Chicano cultural center.

## Midnight Basketball (MBL)—G. Van Standifer, Glenarden, MD, 1986

League games take place from 10:00 p.m. to 2:00 a.m., when temptations to engage in crime and drug activity are greatest. The program has proven effective in helping young men develop self-esteem, gain the skills and the drive to finish school, get GEDs, further their education, learn trades, or find employment. It also gives them the self-respect and inner strength to avoid drugs and resist criminal activity.

## Tenacity—Ned Eames, Boston, MA, 1999

Eames uses his background in tennis to reach students in danger of dropping out of high school by teaching tennis and literacy. Kids meet three or four times a week for three-hour sessions of tennis and studying English and language arts. Summer sessions run as well. The program's goal is to strengthen academic performance, and students in the program have a significantly higher high school graduation rate than average in Boston.

## Experience Aviation—Barrington Irving, Miami, Florida, 2005

Irving saw the convergence between an industry that needed young talent and kids on the streets with nothing to do. Combining education, entrepreneurship, and his extensive background in aviation, he created a nonprofit learning center that introduces children to the joy of flying.

## After School Drill Team—Willie Ellington Bell, Kansas City, MO 2008

When Bell noticed that there were no extracurricular activities at Blenheim Elementary, he created a drill team. The program fosters discipline and has helped with behavioral problems and academics; parents from other schools have requested participation for their children.

## 9th Street Youth Golf Academy—Charlie Seymour, San Bernardino, CA, 1997

After he retired, Seymour devoted his time and much of his pension to creating a youth golf academy for children in San Bernardino's low-income areas. The program was to combine academic tutoring with lessons from golf: self-discipline, honesty, self-control, perseverance, and attention to detail. Thirteen acres of donated land were enough to create a three-hole golf course/learning center. Although Seymour died prior to the completion of the academy, his idea and planning still serves as a project model.

## GlassRoots Nifty Program—Pat Kettenring, Newark, NJ, 2001

This program offers classes in flameworking, kilnforming, lampworking, casting, and glassblowing at little or no cost for at-risk youth in exchange for volunteering or interning. Students learn patience, teamwork, discipline, and business skills as they progress from making beads to blowing glass. They write business plans for the products they produce, present them to business leaders in the community, and attend art shows to sell their works.

## Mural Arts Program—Jane Golden, Philadelphia, PA, 1984

Golden empowered graffiti artists to take active roles in beautifying their neighborhoods by telling their stories and passing on culture and tradition. The Mural Arts Program engages thousands of at-risk children, youth, and adults in free programs that teach transferable life and job skills such as taking personal responsibility, teamwork, and creative problem solving. Their educational programs in prisons and rehabilitation centers use the restorative power of art to break the cycle of crime and violence in communities.

## Knowledge Is Power Program (KIPP)—David Levin and Michael Feinberg, Houston, TX, 1995

KIPP is a national network of open-enrollment and free college-prep public schools. Under contracts signed by students, parents, and teachers, students from low-income families in underserved communities go to school from

7:30 a.m. to 5 p.m. on weekdays, every other Saturday morning, and for an extra month in the summer. In a "no excuses" culture of strict discipline, they earn or lose points toward a weekly "paycheck" that can be cashed in for books or T-shirts at the school store or used toward a weeklong field trip. KIPP has a track record of outstanding high-school graduation rates, and a high percentage of its students go on to college.

## Spark Program—Chris Balme and Melia Dicker, San Francisco, CA, 2004

Spark connects volunteer professionals with middle school students from disadvantaged communities in one-on-one workplace apprenticeships. Students identify a "dream job," apprentice with a mentor in that line of work, and take a leadership class that connects the apprenticeship with learning in school. As students explore the school-to-career connection, the relevance of their education is strengthened, motivating students to work hard to achieve their dreams. The overwhelming majority of students who apprentice go on to college.

## The Three Doctors Foundation—Sampson Davis, Rameck Hunt, George Jenkins, Newark, NJ, 2002

As teenage boys growing up on tough, inner-city streets, they made a pact to stick together, go to college, graduate, and become doctors. Serving as inspirational models of achievement, they stress qualities of self-reliance and inner strength and a strategy of surrounding yourself with like-minded people with similar aspirations. Their premise is that children need to see models that support their aspirations.

## YouthBuild—Dorothy Stoneman, East Harlem, NY, 1978

When Stoneman asked low-income teens what they would do for their communities, they said they would take back abandoned houses from drug dealers, restore them, and give them to homeless families. Today, nationwide, YouthBuild students work full-time on developing workplace skills and completing GEDs or high school graduation requirements. This program integrates employment, housing, crime prevention, leadership development, and community service as students learn construction trades, landscaping, facilities management, and other skills. After up to twenty-four months of training, students head to college, jobs, or both.

## Knitting Together a Community—Judith Symonds, Maplewood, NJ, 2002

Originally conceived as a winter recess activity, this program continued throughout the year. Elementary-school children as young as six participate. Students make friendships as they mentor their peers in knitting skills with the support of adults. The program teaches children success through persistence, concentration, control, follow-through, and mastery while improving fine-motor skills and hand-eye coordination.

## Needle Arts Mentoring Program—Marilyn North and Bonnie Lively, Seaside, OR, 1997

Created for at-risk middle school students, the program promotes problem solving, critical thinking, and creativity. Caring, one-on-one relationships develop between adults and youth as they work on needle arts. Afghan squares for donation to charities are often first projects.

The foregoing examples from my personal collection, no doubt, fall short of the whole of projects in the topic area of mentoring youth, but they illustrate the depth of models in just one area. A national community checklist of projects organized by topics would allow us to see the wealth of our resources along with specific steps we could take to address topics in our communities. For this particular topic, city officials might focus on programs to address the presence of gangs, while some senior citizens might find inspiration to start knitting groups with youth. Others may join with youth to create new projects based on personal interests. The response may be eclectic or ordered—the more influences, the greater the influx of health and inspiration in our communities.

## SERVICE LEARNING: THE INCLUSION OF OUR CHILDREN

In the early years of Charlotte's project, I often wondered why community service projects of value were not more widely replicated. I discovered we had a service learning coordinator for the state of New York, who told me service learning was, in fact, what I had been doing with Charlotte in her project and suggested I attend some service learning conferences to interact with others involved in this work.

I met students and teachers immersed in significant service to their communities as part of their educational curricula. The teachers found service learning to be a manageable part of their teaching load, and they were inspired by the increased motivation among students in their classrooms and personally gratified by the outcomes in their communities. The work was enjoyable, not burdensome.

Inspired by such encounters, I designed a course for first-year college students: "The Human Spirit in Action: Service Learning," in which we created Food2Share, a service learning project that addressed local food insecurity. We replicated components from other food-garnering projects, incorporated a service learning structure, and collected over 4,600 pounds of perishable food in the first year.

## What Is Service Learning?

Service learning is exactly what the term implies: a merger of service work with learning. Teachers identify specific curricular objectives to be addressed through meeting a community need; they design lesson plans based on the subject areas they teach.

Service learning involves four simple structural components to ensure learning through real-life problem solving, responsible endeavor, leadership opportunities, reflection, and developing ongoing relationships and projects in a community near or in another part of the world:

- **Preparation**: The first step involves identifying a significant community need, dialoguing with community-based organizations or personnel in positions of knowledge and authority, gathering information, and planning a problem-solving approach that includes multiple perspectives and sustainable outcomes.
- **Action**: The action phase, as determined in the preparation stage, may involve direct contact with community members in need; indirect work with organizations whose staff work directly with clients; or advocacy to stimulate new perspectives, actions, and

outcomes. (Community service, in contrast to service learning, typically involves only the action component determined by someone in charge of the community-based organization or service event.)

- **Reflection**: Reflection on outcomes and problem-solving decisions made in the preparation phase stimulate critical thinking. Projections in the preparation stage have now become concrete, often implying new goals or direction for future work. Reflection can involve writing, journaling, or class discussion that explores how well the community need is being met, future problem-solving ideas, sustainability, and how the need and problem-solving effort relates to one's own life, other communities, or the broader world.

- **Celebration**: Celebrating the outcome of a project with a larger community audience strengthens recognition of project value and provides inspiration to continue building on the project success. Celebrations can include school-wide assemblies, news articles, radio broadcasts, flyers, and posters. Ongoing projects with yearly celebrations that track outcomes demonstrate sustainability.

Service learning projects create solutions for community needs and experiential learning for students. One of the striking aspects of service learning is that youth seem almost driven to learn because it's fun when it's attached to real life; they want to gain the necessary skills to carry out activities and work with peers and teachers. Service learning strengthens the desire to learn and the sense of one's person in relation to others and the world, and this provides a variety of ways to "shine" beyond traditional academic assessment methods. Success is a positive experience; failure requires additional problem-solving effort.

Service learning projects stimulate cooperative learning that provides enrichment and variety for an educational system based primarily on individual achievement. The youth I have observed seem to have very little if any interest in external praise from adults. Their attention is totally focused on the work itself. Being absorbed by a task and meeting a genuine need are fulfilling. Students get to know each other while discovering their individual strengths. Student learning in this context is not burdensome, and motivation runs high, creating a positive learning environment for everyone that spills over into other academic subjects. Terry Pickerel, a senior consultant to the Education Commission of the States (www.infousa.state.gov), puts it this way:

> A variety of research studies have concluded that quality service learning has a decidedly positive impact on students. They demonstrate that this phenomenon leads to improved academic performance, gains in knowledge of the service provided, growth in higher order thinking, expanded social and civic responsibility, increased acceptance of cultural diversity, and enhanced self-esteem. Ultimately, it is engagement, not mere exposure, that counts.

Service learning projects join curricular learning components with civic engagement. Government officials are seeking solutions for community needs and ways to support the education of our youth. Teachers are seeking cooperation and motivation from youth in the classroom. Parents are seeking signs that their children are engaging in their education—that they are learning and happy. Service learning meets all these objectives.

## FOOD2SHARE: A SERVICE LEARNING PROJECT

After a presentation Charlotte gave to our local United Way, the director remarked to me on how she wished there was something her organization could do about the food problem in our community. Like many community members, I was aware of periodic canned food drives, holiday meals, and the occasional donation one could make at a grocery store checkout, but her comment revealed these initiatives were not meeting this community need.

Unsure of a solution, I searched online for models and found a perishable food-garnering program active in over 100 schools in Tampa Bay, Florida. The program, started by David Levitt as part of his bar mitzvah preparation, received its inspiration from USA Harvest, which originated in Kentucky. I talked with David's mother, staff at Tampa Bay schools and Tampa Bay Harvest, and with staff at other perishable food-reclamation programs in Atlanta and Kansas City.

With materials from these programs in hand and a group of college students I was leading in a course entitled "The Human Spirit in Action:

Service Learning," we began to organize replication in our community. Working with corporate food service, restaurants, two colleges, and our public schools, and adapting to overcome significant challenges, we created a comprehensive service learning program: Food2Share. The basic outline of how Food2Share works in a K-12 district-wide model is as follows:

- Students learn what foods can be donated and those that must be thrown out. (For example, unopened bags of chips or carrot sticks are acceptable, but opened ones are not.)
- Coolers near waste collection areas in school cafeterias allow students to separate food for donation from waste.
- Food collected goes to food banks that weigh and record it and report back to the schools.
- In addition to food contributed by students, food service leftovers frozen in good-quality, gallon-freezer bags become a major contribution to food banks. While food-service personnel work to reduce excess food, they can't always predict food consumption. They, however, can freeze leftovers for volunteer transport to the food bank.

The joint efforts of students and staff create community bonding that affects morale in the school environment; everyone is able to find a role in solution making. This is how the service learning structure played out in the college course:

## Preparation

The preparation phase involved researching materials that were integral to the design of other models:

- EPA: Food Donation: Feed Families, Not Landfills
  www.epa.gov
- Emerson Good Samaritan Food Donation Act
  www.feedingamerica.org
- USDA: A Citizen's Guide to Food Recovery
  www.usda.gov
- Food service guidelines from the Tampa Bay-area public schools

The director of our local food bank discussed the materials and models we had found in class. He was so inspired by the possibilities the students were bringing to help solve the problem of food insecurity that he wanted to work with the students and began attending the class. I realized my students were functioning as volunteer staff furthering his problem-solving efforts.

The goal in the beginning stages was to replicate food service donations as done in Tampa Bay-area schools: when the last student is served, food service staff freezes excess food in good-quality freezer bags until transport by parent volunteers. A meeting with a representative from our department of health confirmed Tampa Bay's food service guidelines.

## Action

Some of my students approached the college's food service director, who conferred with the corporate office and scheduled a meeting with kitchen staff, who were eager to help. They offered suggestions to create work flow for this component. An e-mail to all professors quickly produced a volunteer pool for transport. One student created a volunteer schedule and an e-mail distribution list among the volunteers to sustain communication and food transportation. Excess prepared food from the college kitchen began to flow to our food bank.

Some students solicited restaurants, and the owner of one exceeded their expectations. Elena's Sweet Indulgence was a small café that served salads, warm entrees, bread, and desserts, and its owner started donating leftovers at the end of each day that she put in individual serving-size microwavable containers. When the food bank director learned of her contribution, he told the students the food was potentially lifesaving, as many older residents were not inspired to make meals of canned food, while this food was appetizing.

Other students approached the public school food service with the food service donation model from Tampa Bay schools. The director of our public school food service committed to the project after conferring with the K-12 department at the corporate office. Everything was set to go for the following fall in our public schools, including a donation of freezer bags from a store.

Change, a real-life element, jostled the project when our public school food service director retired that summer. A new class of first-year students was ready to build on the work of the previous year's students, but the new public school food service director for our community informed us that the program could not happen. Our public schools happened to be under contract with the same corporate entity as our college food service; this corporation had separate offices for different areas of service. Although the corporate college food service department supported the project, as did the corporate community relations office, the individual in charge of the corporate K-12 food service would not support the project and aggressively took steps to shut down our efforts.

We were never able to get this component off the ground in our public schools. We could find no difference between the college and public school kitchens, as staff trained in food handling were operating both. Our college food service continued to make regular donations, but my students were predictably dismayed by what they perceived to be poor role modeling in the adult professional world and that a single individual could block the logical and positive flow of giving from so many to those in need.

Nonetheless, I was working with youth—resilient college students— who were pursuing a course in service learning. We had an agenda to problem solve. Despite this one stumbling block, we still had support in the community; everyone involved had been perplexed by this turn of events, including our superintendent and principals.

Up to this point, both classes of first-year college students had been pursuing food service donations. We turned our attention to the portion of David Levitt's project that addressed unopened milks from students in the cafeteria and extended this to wrapped snacks and whole fruits, as suggested by our food bank director.

We worked with our superintendent, principals, teachers, students, parents, and lunch aides. Everyone got onboard, restoring our faith in community and possibilities for solutions. Our children were eager for inclusion, and our lunch aides felt their presence in the cafeteria increased in value. Our superintendent told us the program supported his work in representing the outcomes of education to the community.

This class of college students took charge of meetings with the department of health, school principals, and parent teacher organization members to generate volunteers to transport food. They made posters for school cafeterias and presented the model to students at school assemblies. Kindergartners took on the task of putting up the Food2Share signs in cafeterias, and older students took charge of transferring food from the cafeteria collection bin to a refrigerated cooler. As our children learned, they stepped forward to contribute. They were an inspirational antidote to the corporate rejection, bringing immediacy of action and purity of vision.

## Reflection

As my college students spent time with cafeteria aides and parents, they returned with quotes in their journals, including these we received from lunch aides:

- "There is so much food waste. I've seen it for years, and it's always upset me."
- "It's a relief to know the food is not going in the garbage."
- "This is a great idea!"

A parent transport volunteer gave us a telling comment as well: "I have really enjoyed working with this project and feel it is so needed. My son is getting a grasp of what it is and what it does. In a day and age where kids have too much, something like this shows them it's not that way for everyone."

A sixth-grade teacher used Food2Share as the topic for a reflective writing assignment that involved writing about the Food2Share program. The following are excerpts from the students' personal responses:

- "The program prevents us from throwing away perfectly good food, and it goes to the people who need it more than we do."
- "It is the easiest way for a person in elementary school to help someone."
- "I'm glad our school is participating in the Food2Share program because it's an opportunity to help make Oneonta a better place to live."
- "A lot of children give food every day, and I think that this is really something to be proud of! Everyone at our school loves this program."
- "I think the Food2Share program is a great way to save food and give other people the food that you were going to throw out. I

learned you shouldn't throw away food you are not going to eat!
Save the food for someone who needs it."

- "I think this program should be in schools all around the United States. I hope that after you read this you will be raising food with the Food2Share program."
- "Anyone can make a difference. Food2Share just makes sharing a little easier!"
- "I believe Food2Share is one of the best programs that have come to our town. We are donating clean and fresh food to our fellow citizens. It makes me proud to know I might be helping to save someone's life or keep them healthier by giving food I'm not going to eat."

As outcomes took shape, inspiration grew among my students. A service learning structure was forming for students in the elementary schools. We had incorporated preparation, action, and reflection, and we headed for celebration. As often happens in service learning projects, more ideas surfaced. The food bank began to send monthly donation statistics, broken down for each school and the college.

*Sandy McKane*

SHAW CLIFTON
GENERAL

LAWRENCE R. MORETZ
TERRITORIAL COMMANDER

# THE SALVATION ARMY
FOUNDED IN 1865 BY WILLIAM BOOTH

**ONEONTA CORPS**
25 RIVER STREET
ONEONTA, N.Y. 13820-2340
PHONE (607) 432-5960
FAX (607) 441-7311

August 16, 2007

Sandy McKane

Oneonta, NY 13820

Dear Sandy:

The poundage for the month of March, 2007 is as follows:

| | | | |
|---|---|---|---|
| Center Street School | 69 lbs | 10 oz | $34.55 |
| Hartwick College | 151 lbs | 4 oz | $75.52 |
| Oneonta Middle School | 30 lbs | 11 oz | $15.05 |
| Riverside School | 44 lbs | 2 oz | $22.01 |
| Valleyview School | 65 lbs | 2 oz | $32.51 |
| Elena's Sweet Indulgence | 174 lbs | | $87.00 |
| | | | $266.64 |

The number of households we helped with food in March, 2007 was 188 and there were 535 individuals.

Thank you and may God bless you.

Sincerely,

*Sharon Haines*

Sharon Haines

A United Way Agency

*A bequest to The Salvation Army will perpetuate your interest.*

We also received responses from the staff at the food bank:

- "Milk is rare. It's wonderful to get and a lot of people ask for it, and we can't provide it usually."

- "The milk is fantastic—much better than powdered milk. It's a great present. Please tell the children the families are thrilled."
- "It's been impossible for us to do fresh milk. There were 200 families this month, 579 individuals."

A fifth-grade teacher requested the food donation statistics for use in a graphing unit students were studying in math. After several days of graphing exercises, students explored a website for graph making. After the students made a graph with only their school's data, the teacher had students try to figure out how to add the donation data from the other schools and told us, "They did this with no problem. The students loved it and asked to go back to do more."

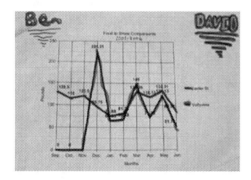 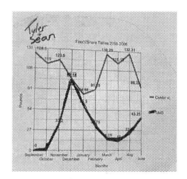

Another teacher offered to have her students create an updatable graph for the cafeteria. One teacher weighed in with the comment, "I never thought about it; we collect food at certain times of the year, but the need is year 'round." In addition, the rural health director told us, "This program puts a face on food insecurity that a centralized system can't. There are more relationships."

## Celebration

A school-wide assembly at the beginning of the year was the perfect time to share the previous year's outcomes and kick off the start of the new year. Food bank representatives shared the need in the community and the value of the students' actions and contributions. A newspaper article and radio broadcast informed the community of the contribution students were making to address food insecurity in the community.

Greater awareness resulted; community members called to ask if they could donate leftovers from concession stands or catered events. Food bank representatives, trained in food handling, were able to provide the support required to make this happen.

Some of my college students, faced with significant leftovers from a weekend event, made calls to get the food expeditiously transported to our homeless shelter because the food bank was closed. Their classroom learning had made its way out into the larger framework of their lives, and their excitement for having recognized this opportunity was overwhelmingly present as they shared this outcome in class.

In our community, with four elementary schools, one middle school, a college food service, and a restaurant contributing to the formation of Food2Share, we collected over 16,000 pounds in four years. Although food insecurity was the originating focus for Food2Share, the program also diverted a significant amount of organic waste from our landfills. The value of service work taken into the educational arena provided real-life experiential learning that met a real community need.

# PART TWO

▼

# "By the People"

We can organize our contributions and work more efficiently to reach everyone by creating a comprehensive model that draws together existing solutions to embrace the full scope of the world, a model that continues to incorporate new solutions evolving from the best of our capabilities.

## A NATIONAL K-12 SERVICE CURRICULUM

When and how do we include our youth in the search for answers to our large-scale challenges? When and how do we begin an educational process that helps them address the varied, complex needs in our world? Adults often refer to children as the hope of the world, but if our youth are to make large-scale, needful changes, we need to assess our success in educating them to solve problems at this level in the real world. Logic will eventually turn us to the earliest developmental and foundational period of growth.

Our children are part of "the people." Our children have suggested and created outstanding service models at home as well as abroad. They are the next generation and will create the future for those who follow. If we hesitate to include our children in collective problem solving, we should consider the high value that gangs—or the global equivalent, terrorists—find in collecting our youth for violent and destructive activity. These groups recognize and capitalize on the desire of youth to become part of a larger community and purpose. We can create a conversely focused structure for our youth based on constructive values of peace, productivity, and caring for others and the environment.

What would it be like if all our children regularly engaged in community service? How powerful would their contributions be if they communicated with their peers nationwide at the same grade levels and worked on replicable models of service in their communities? What would it be like for all communities to engage simultaneously in outstanding project models, helping those in need and restoring the environment? What would happen if we looked to our children for solutions and respected the support they bring to our world? What would we see if we consistently looked through the lens of our children's vision? How would they feel about their education and their place in the world? How would project originators feel to see their work spun out nationwide and worldwide? How would a generation of adults interact, having grown together in making the world a better place, with quantifiable results and well-established working relationships? What would it be like if every school district had a sister-city relationship in a developing area of the world? What if all community members knew that schools managed a checklist of community projects with specific project information?

Is this possible? Absolutely!

What would our standing in the world be if we set the standard for working together to create lasting change, honoring future generations of adults in their formative stages of growth—if we became the central axis for information and collective work worldwide, with all our children at the helm?

Could we sustain this? Absolutely!

Americans are perfectly suited for this megachange. We have always been able to see the possibilities and create a future that embraces many from diverse backgrounds. Our schools are the perfect sustainable vehicle for staffing this change at home and abroad. We simply need to reorganize our problem-solving methods and transition into a new realm of history for the human race.

A K-12 service learning curriculum, implemented nationally, would add a critical developmental component to the Serve America Act (www. nationalservice.gov), addressing community needs while developing civic competencies—beginning in the youngest grade levels. The K-12 model also establishes participation in the global community through interaction with, and support of, sister cities.

Accumulated outcomes would create new and relevant validity for the time students spend in school every day, every year. Our children would have evidence that education is valuable and that they are valuable. They would be linked with adults and peers nationwide and globally, all working and achieving "on the same page" to make the world a better place. They would enter our communities as adults with problem-solving experience and know how to make a difference in ongoing ways, with action-based cooperative problem solving as a way of life.

## K-12 SERVICE LEARNING OUTLINE

Service learning projects show up mostly in middle and high schools, with very few in elementary schools. Conversely, I started a service learning project with my daughter Charlotte when she was entering kindergarten. Inspired by the strength of service learning to motivate children to learn and create needed outcomes in the community, I approached elementary school teachers in my community. Grade by grade, I worked with teachers to create age-appropriate service learning projects that would trace experiential learning and leadership roles, beginning with kindergarten. The goal was to sustain a thread of experiential learning through graduation in a well-conceived, sequenced, and integrated curriculum—developed among ourselves as Americans.

My idea of a K-12 national service learning curriculum would include:

- Grade-specific educational service projects that support community needs
- A checklist of community projects managed by our schools
- A sister-city relationship between every community in the United States and a developing global community
- Outstanding, field-tested project models
- Communication, prioritization, and ongoing project development
- Sequenced leadership roles for our children

## SPECIFIC MODELS IN SPECIFIC GRADES

Distinct from other areas of study, a service learning curriculum would be most effective as a nationally coordinated effort that would have a framework of grade-specific projects in elementary school. From a young age, students would gain inspiration by their contributions, joining with their peers nationwide.

If specific projects are matched with specific grade levels, younger students can look forward to projects they have seen older students manage, anticipate activities and leadership roles, and build on the work of previous classes. Older students can mentor younger students and contribute advanced components to projects managed by younger students.

The premise is to begin with simple, signature projects in early grades and expand with more-complex project components in middle school and high school. Beginning experimentation has revealed the following possibilities for sequenced, grade-specific project areas and leadership roles that begin in kindergarten:

- Kindergarten—Animal Shelters
- 1st Grade—Hospitals
- 2nd Grade—Shelters
- 3rd Grade—Sister Cities
- 4th Grade—Disabilities
- 5th Grade—Food Banks
- 6th Grade—Recycling
- 7th-12th Grades:
  o Continuation of Food2Share and Recycling
  o Environmental Issues
  o Expansion of project areas supported by a national checklist of projects

# K-12 Snapshot

What would it look like if we followed the path of our youth grade by grade through a K-12 service learning curriculum? With leadership projects at each grade level, the school year begins with the responsibility of presenting information to the class a grade level below and receiving information from the class a grade ahead. Passing leadership roles on from grade to grade becomes a tradition and expectation among students, signifying their progression in responsibility and leadership.

## Kindergarten

Kindergartners learn about Caring for Animals from first graders. Following service learning preparation components, kindergartners take charge of communications with an animal shelter, updating the community checklist with needed items, receiving donations and supplies from community members, and adding local outcomes to a nationwide database in which they join with nationwide peers engaged in the same leadership roles in their communities. When it is time for reflection on their project work, older grade buddies assist kindergartners with their first written service learning journal entry.

Kindergartners participate in Food2Share and recycling and learn of other grades' projects through assembly celebrations during which they share the results of their first community leadership role in the Caring for Animals project.

## First Grade

First graders present their work in Caring for Animals to the kindergartners and also receive information about their new leadership roles for the hospital dolls project from second graders who managed the project the previous year.

After visiting with hospital staff and learning about the purpose of hospital dolls, first graders engage in creating an ongoing supply of the dolls based on hospitals' needs. The new responsibility for monthly communication with the hospital reiterates the process and importance of communication with the animal shelter in Caring for Animals. First graders combine their local outcomes with peers nationwide, who progress with them into this new leadership role in their communities.

First graders continue in regular routines established by Food2Share and the recycling program and increase their understanding of other service learning projects through celebration assemblies.

## Second Grade

Second graders continue in Food2Share and recycling and take on the project of assembling gift bags for children and teens at safe houses who have brought few if any personal belongings. A visit with an educator from the Violence Intervention Program increases students' awareness of the provision for shelter in their communities and the variety of support components that can help.

## Third Grade

By third grade, students will have come to know of their sister city through fund-raising celebrations, projects that highlight the cultural aspects of their sister city, and perhaps, T-shirts that document progress from year to year. They learn in greater detail and build on the work of students who preceded them.

Communication with peers nationwide expands to include third-graders in their sister city in a developing area of the world—a relationship that continues over the course of their education as they progress toward graduation and next steps in life.

## Fourth Grade

In the Disabilities Awareness service learning project, students experience for themselves what they have seen previous classes of students do. Each student has the opportunity to spend one full school day in a wheelchair. Although this is a new experience, problem-solving needs in different life circumstances has become a familiar theme in their education. As they engage in critical thinking and interaction with people with disabilities, they discover new perspectives of accessibility and mobility in their physical environment.

## Fifth Grade

Ownership of Food2Share heightens students' awareness of how the whole community can come together to create solutions. Fifth graders get statistics from the food bank that list school, grocery store, and restaurant donations as well as donations from community members at grocery stores. With this information, they create graphs and post them in their cafeterias and at grocery stores.

## Sixth Grade

Sixth graders work with waste management personnel to discuss national checklist models and possible improvements to existing community recycling processes. As a graduating class, they transfer their leadership role at the end of the year to fifth graders.

## Grades Seven through Twelve

Students who have progressed through a sequence of service learning projects that were not simply units of study, but leadership responsibilities spanning every year, bring different expectations, skills, and energy to middle school. They and the larger community come to see the elementary grade school years as the foundation on which everything builds.

One of the differences in students who emerge from this foundation of community-building work is that they will have interacted with adults in the community and will have received information from older students and shared projects with younger students. They will have broken through the artificial barriers that would separate them by age. These young adults in middle school can support younger peers in project work in which they have also engaged; they can now assess more needs and ways to further strengthen their communities as they consider, with their teachers, the broader scope and depth of solutions available in a checklist of national projects.

# Kindergarten: Caring for Animals

Kindergarten teachers in our community identified animals as the starting point for a community leadership role. Kindergartners learn leadership and contribution by managing the collection of items for animal care throughout the year. The goal, as with all service learning projects, is to develop an ongoing, long-term relationship with the community-based organization, in this case, an animal shelter.

After a visit with animal shelter staff, the leadership role for kindergartners begins with monthly communication with the animal shelter to obtain a list of needed items. Students inform the community and gather supplies. Sustaining the project throughout the year and from year to year educates all students and community members that kindergartners are managing these needed donations. Instead of an annual drive for items that can overwhelm community-based organizations and leave them without help at other times, an ongoing relationship continues from month to month, providing a steady stream of awareness as well as support.

With a service learning model in place nationwide, kindergartners would lay a foundation for shared work and communication with their peers from all parts of the country. They would build relationships with their peers, sharing what they are learning, refining best practices, and combining their community contribution statistics to create national outcomes.

They would also begin to experience from early on their value in the community, the support education brings to their ability to engage and contribute, and the support they can bring to one another as they meet the needs of our animal shelters, together, nationwide.

## Materials

Ingredients and supplies to make dog biscuits and catnip toys

## Service Learning Outline:

## Preparation

Animal shelter representatives speak with students about dog safety, kindness to animals, and the role of the shelter in the community. Students learn about the work of veterinarians in their community. They read fiction and nonfiction books about dogs and cats.

## Action

Students request a "wish list" of needed items from the animal shelter each month and work to gather the needed items, which typically include food, blankets, or worn-out towels, collars, leashes, and cleaning supplies. They update the community checklist with this information and manage donations for delivery to the shelter. They also make dog biscuits and catnip toys for animals in the shelter.

## Reflection

Group discussion along with drawing and story writing allow students to express what they have learned about animals, how to care for them, and how the community can support the work of the animal shelter. Graphing activities include picture graphs of pets students have at home, a Venn diagram to compare and contrast differences and similarities between cats and dogs, and a graph to track donated items.

## Celebration

Students contact and inform news media of the project. A flyer is created for parents and the community to learn about the outcomes of the project, inviting them to a school-wide assembly during which the project and its results are presented. The event could be scheduled during Be Kind to Animals Week in May.

## Disciplines Incorporated

- Language Arts
- Art
- Mathematics
- Health/Safety

## Responses

The response from our local SPCA was that this was a "terrific project." Nearby community shelters wanted to be included, and one teacher told us, "Every year it gets easier, and we expand to include more things. Now we are focusing on why animals are important. We're creating journals for the students to draw and write."

## Expansion

Additional support suggested by our shelter that older students or community members could provide included:

- Adoption booklets based on what the students learn
- Flyers for animals in need of adoption
- Walking dogs at the shelter
- Training dogs at the shelter

**Additional presentation topic possibilities**

- Police dogs
- Dogs for the blind
- Rescue dogs

# First Grade: Hospital Dolls

A project for first graders was the next consideration for a K-12 service learning sequence. The main criteria were curriculum and genuine community need. Teachers suggested a project with hospitals, since first graders already visit with hospital staff as part of a health unit of study.

I had a number of service projects in my database collection under the topic of hospitals; however, when I contacted our hospital, emergency room nurses requested "hospital dolls." Unsure of what these were, I searched online and found the "hospital dolls" that Kiwanis of Burnside, Australia, had created. With a match between curriculum and community need, we also discovered that our first graders were the perfect age to understand this need.

We found hospitals in Maryland, Tennessee, Michigan, Pennsylvania, and California that used such dolls. With instructions from Kiwanis and additional information from the hospitals, we created a service learning project for first graders. Our emergency room nurses were enthusiastic about our taking on this project.

The premise for the dolls is that a hospital experience can be an overwhelming experience for a child. Any injury that sends a child to the emergency room is aggravated by bright lights, strange noises, unfamiliar equipment, and strangers who take away clothes and poke and prod; a child hurts and has no sense of control, but a hospital doll can comfort them. The dolls are blank—they have no facial features. The children get a pen or a nontoxic permanent marker to draw faces on their dolls, which allows them to express their feelings and personalize the dolls—a pleasant and distracting activity.

The purpose of the dolls, however, is more far-reaching. The doll is less threatening as a form of communication for young children who may be fearful of or resistant to treatment. Children who may initially be uncooperative or uncommunicative start relaxing and engaging with hospital staff when they have one of these dolls. The child can mark the area of injury and the pain they feel and can more easily share feelings and concerns through the doll, which helps staff make assessments. As staff develop rapport with a child, they can use the doll to explain procedures and help prepare the child for a treatment or test. Staff can use the doll to show where they will be giving injections or a posture or a desired body position they want the child to assume. Children become more cooperative and cope more effectively with the doll as a source of comfort. After treatment, children can dress the dolls and take them home.

## Materials

- Muslin or cotton with no sheen so markers can be used on the fabric
- Light, middle, and dark skin shades
- One yard of 45" fabric will yield three dolls
- Stuffing

Retail cost (in 2007) for fifty dolls:

- 12 yards for 36 cream-colored dolls @ .99 per yard = $12
- 5 yards for 15 darker-colored dolls @ $1.99 per yard = $10
- 50-pound box of stuffing: $14
- Total $36

## Service Learning Outline:

## Preparation

First graders visit with hospital staff to learn about health, routine examinations, and equipment used. They also learn how staffers use the dolls and the value of this contribution.

## Sewing Component

First graders were old enough to understand the purpose of the dolls and to stuff them, but they were not old enough to sew them. The construction of the dolls involves simple cutting and sewing around edges with curves. The opening for stuffing needs to allow for first graders to stuff the doll with ease, and it is important to stay on the pattern, as misshapen dolls are hard to use at the hospital. After first graders stuff the dolls, the openings need to be sewn up. Hospital gowns with arms and Velcro at the neck can also be made from donated scraps.

Our high school Family Career and Community Leaders of America (FCCLA) students took on this sewing task with this response: "We are looking forward to direct involvement with the first graders and definitely want to be involved with the first graders when it is time to stuff the dolls." These high school students were excited to have a reason to work with first graders on a community service project, and the first graders were excited to have the high school students come to their class with the dolls for them to stuff and dress. Creating partnerships and working together was clearly enriching for both groups. In the absence of such a connection, another possibility for this support task could be community members who sew. An after-school program could serve as an alternate location for sewing the dolls.

## Action

First graders stuff the dolls, starting with the head, then arms and legs, chest last. Dolls should be plump but not stiff so the dolls can bend although not flop. Original instructions included chopsticks to stuff the dolls, but our first graders were able to stuff the dolls better with just their fingers. When the dolls were completed, first graders dressed the dolls.

Monthly communications with the hospital keep first graders updated on the need for more dolls, mirroring the sustained relationship first graders had with the animal shelter in kindergarten.

## Reflection

This is typically a written activity after discussion about the purpose and significance of the contribution.

## Celebration

At a school-wide assembly, a representative from the hospital shares project outcomes and first graders share reflection excerpts. Newspaper articles and radio station spots inform the community of the event.

## Disciplines incorporated

- Health
- Language Arts

## Responses from our hospital

- "The dolls have been awesome! The nurses love them and use them all the time."
- "A two-year-old girl came into the emergency room the other day needing stitches. She was scared and weepy. As soon as she got the doll, she settled right down. She loved the doll and put Band-Aids all over it. She even put a Band-Aid on the spot where her own blood had dripped."

In less than a month, the first delivery of dolls to the hospital from one class was almost gone. Our hospital provided us with the number of children who would benefit from the dolls annually. In our community, 450 children between the ages of one and eight go through the emergency room each year. This kind of information allows for planning that spans the entire year, with monthly updates from the hospital.

## Expansion

A national checklist of projects from many communities nationwide would provide a wide variety of support for local hospital staff to consider. Older students or community members could generate these support projects. The following are some project possibilities from my database collection:

- Holiday placemats
- Activity bags

- DVDs and books
- Murals and artwork
- Cards for children with serious illnesses
- Visitations
- Personalized T-shirts for ventilator patients
- Pillows for heart patients to buffer the pain of coughing
- Hats for cancer patients
- Handmade clothing, hats, and blankets for premature babies

In addition to providing hospital dolls as their signature project, first graders also serve as the liaison between monthly requests from the hospital and donations from the community. Hospitals gain a reliable community contact, duplication of more well-known needs is reduced, and the variety of support increases. Over time, community members come to know that first graders manage this connection, honoring the work of these young but capable youth, and contributing to hospitals and also to the education of our youth.

## Second Grade: Violence Intervention Safe House Gift Bags

The elementary teachers with whom I worked were not necessarily service learning advocates, but they expressed interest in service projects for their students. Having become a service learning advocate wanting to create a sequence of projects in elementary grades, I served as a facilitator between teachers with service interests and community organizations. A second-grade teacher in one of our elementary schools asked for help with a service project of gathering items for a toiletry drive for our Violence Intervention Program (VIP) safe house. As facilitator, I initiated conversation with VIP staff, looking for a service learning connection.

The suggestion of toiletry items met with a positive response from VIP staff. However, I knew from other project work, that this was offering a solution before asking them for their needs, so I asked staff for other possible areas that could also become the focus of the project. After some discussion, a staff member shared that VIP routinely received toiletry items from a variety of community members and organizations. She described the children who arrive at the safe house with nothing more than the clothes on their backs and maybe a favorite blanket. The toys at the safe house were communal, so the children had few if any personal possessions.

We came up with a preliminary plan to make bags filled with age- and gender-appropriate things for the children at the safe house. The second-grade teacher realized the educational value this new project focus could bring to her students. Service learning tends to have an infectious quality those involved in service learning know well. The second-grade teacher's enthusiasm spilled over beyond her classroom as she reached out to a middle school home and careers teacher, seeing a point of curricular convergence. The middle school teacher mirrored her enthusiasm, suggesting that her students could make drawstring bags for their sewing unit, and she personally contributed the fabric for the project.

As teachers come together to work on a genuine community need, ideas flow and converge, increasing involvement and the educational value for our youth. The two teachers created a plan that would bring the grade school class to the middle school, where they would work together to fill the bags. They wanted their students to make a card for each bag with a handprint of the middle school and the elementary school students involved to add a personal touch.

The educator for VIP was particularly pleased. This service learning project created the opportunity for her to visit with students of differing ages and brought a unique focus to her work with them. Service learning provided students with a point of personal engagement and contribution beyond a purely informational encounter with the educator about the work of the VIP in our community. We were weaving an integrated web of service and learning among students and community-based organizations that was inspirationally engaging for everyone.

## Service Learning Outline:

## Preparation

## Second Grade

The educator from VIP visits the second-grade classes to share the purpose of the safe house and the need for items for the children and teens who leave their homes quickly and with very few personal belongings.

Together with the educator, the students brainstorm possible items for the bags, thinking of a child their age or an older brother or sister. The number of children in the safe house over the past year is broken down by age and gender. Second graders choose specific children by age and gender for each bag they will create.

A list of contents on the outside of each bag allows safe house staff to quickly assess its contents and remove anything inappropriate for a specific child.

A letter goes home to students' parents, describing the project and offering them the opportunity to donate items students have identified for the project.

## Middle School

The educator for VIP also visits the middle school home and careers classes, sharing services provided for clients and how collaborative work creates a support system. Students then receive instruction on how to make drawstring bags.

## Action

### Second Grade

Students organize purchased and donated items for each bag. (Our second graders took a trip to the local Dollar Store with $2 each to purchase two items for their bags; our PTO donated the money for this.)

### Middle School

Students measure, cut out, and sew colorful fabric drawstring bags.

### Second Grade and Middle School

Second graders fill the drawstring bags, and middle school students list the items in each bag. Together, students create cards that include their handprints.

## Reflection

The second- and eighth-grade teachers engage their students in reflective dialogue about the project and their participation. Students write about their contribution to the project as well as how the children at the safe house might feel when they receive the gift bags.

## Celebration

The educator from VIP shares the project from the organization's perspective, and students share reflection excerpts at a school-wide assembly. The community learns of the event via newspaper articles and radio spots.

An added bonus for VIP is that this event is another quantifiable educational encounter, which helps the organization qualify for state and federal program funding.

## Disciplines Incorporated

- Language Arts
- Social Studies
- Art

## Responses

The safe house told us, "We don't have any left. They were a big hit here. It would be great if you are doing that project again. We could definitely use them."

The second-grade teacher who had piloted the project changed grades the following year to teach kindergarten. One day she came running down the hall to tell me a kindergartner who had been living at the safe house had come for show and tell with one of the bags. This teacher told me with tears in her eyes that the project had been meaningful at the time with her second graders but had really hit home when this kindergartner came to class with one of the bags.

## Adaptations

What was possible one year for us was not possible the following year, when budget cuts made it impossible for middle school and second graders to meet. Our teachers adapted with immediacy: fifth- and sixth-grade "buddies" assisted the second graders in the shopping process and creating lists for the bags as second graders filled the drawstring bags again created by the middle schoolers.

Adaptations are enriching, and many more would be shared among teachers and students nationwide. The goal is to maintain the essence of a signature project at each grade level while also providing a cohesive point of civic engagement for youth on a national level.

## Expansion

The national checklist of project topics specifically for shelters suggested by my database collection to date have some rather well defined levels of complexity. Simpler projects provide:

- Blankets or quilts as personalized gifts
- School kits
- Books
- Clothing
- Personal necessities such as socks, underwear, and hygiene items
- Birthday bags for youth
- Furniture for transition to homes

Projects with more-involved components that support elders in the community who live alone provide:

- Daily welfare calls
- Assistance with chores
- Emergency information vials (health history, emergency contact information, etc.)

More-complex projects for community leaders to consider under the topic of shelters address:

- Permanent supportive housing
- Homeless women, single parents, teen mothers
- Repairing and rebuilding homes for the elderly and disabled
- Building single-family homes on vacant lots
- Job training programs

As in earlier grades, second graders have a signature project that addresses a specific need related to shelter as a safe haven. Their new leadership role focuses more broadly on all shelters in their community. As the contact point between shelters and community members, they provide monthly updates to the community checklist. In this leadership role, they become educated about the ways communities work to provide shelter for those in need.

## Third Grade: Sister City—A Global Service Learning Component

Is it possible that youth in developed nations and youth in developing areas of the world could come together with purpose? Could they help to restructure our world toward productivity, respect, and peace? Can community-based leadership roles inspire our youth to take an active role in shaping the society they will live in as adults? Can we give them this opportunity?

Any research into the outcomes of service learning to date will head us toward a resounding yes as a response to these questions. Have we, to date, explored this possibility? Not on a large scale. What if every community had a sister-city service learning project? What if global solution-bearing project models were on a checklist for not only our children to study but for actual use based on the needs of their specific sister city? How would our children feel if they were able to work with peers nationwide, combining their global outcomes with a larger picture of global progression, humanitarian and environmental? How would international relations play out over time if our children learned to communicate effectively with others from different backgrounds? Learning from project originators who model the process of listening first and then creating solutions that over time become fully sustainable by the sister city, how would our children feel as they grew into adulthood, having worked together to help one another? What would our world standing look like if this took place? Is it possible that being an American might take on new significance that would bind us together in positive momentum?

Our children's knowledge of geography alone would spike because of relevance created among themselves; they would see their contributions in the larger scope of an ever-changing world—one in which they have direct influence. If every school district had a sister-city relationship, we would lay an incredibly strong foundation for productive, peaceful, global relationships as youth grow.

We are smarter and more compassionate than our current world conditions indicate; we can do better. A simple and actionable sister-city component in a K-12 service learning model provides a way to accomplish more. We owe this to the next generation because we—the current generation—can do so.

## Finding a Sister City

Worldwide organizations create partnerships between areas of need and those who can help. They also sustain communications, track outcomes, and seek support from the general population. A national K-12 service learning office would work with these organizations to set up sister cities with trustworthy project managers.

Project originators and project managers around the world demonstrate it is possible to successfully navigate local politics, processes, and cultural traditions. They work to determine whom to contact, how best to obtain supplies, and how to get genuine buy-in from locals.

A sister-city service learning project as a component of a national K-12 model is comprehensive, long-term, and developmental, and it has the potential to address multiple areas of need over time. This kind of dependable, ongoing support is a perfect match with the ongoing, sustained, committed work of project originators and organizations working with them to replicate long-term solutions where similar needs exist.

## A Global Projects Checklist

Over the past eleven years, in addition to project models in the United States, I have gathered global projects from print and online sources and organized them by topic. Similar to the national checklist, these projects can serve as an accessible resource as we adopt sister cities. Global projects address unique geographic and societal conditions in developing areas of the world that are, most often, distinct from our own communities.

## Global Projects Checklist

### Peace, Reconciliation, Recovery

- Land disputes: Botswana
- Blood feuds: Albania, Lebanon
- Peace tents: Kenya
- Seed distribution ceremonies: Kenya
- Forgiveness: Sierra Leone
- Settling conflicts: Turkey
- Trade: Pakistan, India
- Building roads: Kenya
- Slavery: Brazil, Ghana
- Land mines: Tanzania, Mozambique
- Rape victims: Congo, Jordan
- Widows: Afghanistan
- Music: Iran, Lebanon

### Education

- Daycare: Thailand
- Child labor victims: Pakistan
- Youth as teachers: Brazil, Bangladesh
- Building schools: South Africa, Pakistan, Afghanistan, India, Cambodia
- Libraries: South Africa, Ethiopia, Senegal, Laos, Nepal
- PCs: Laos
- Laptop servers: Mozambique
- Wireless networks: South Asia
- Basketball: Saudi Arabia, South Africa
- Wrestling: India
- Boxing: Brazil
- Dance: Columbia
- Music: Venezuela
- Juggling: Bolivia

### Shelter

- Adoption: South Africa, Guatemala
- Orphanages: Thailand, South Africa, Liberia, Rwanda, China, Syria
- Street children: Philippines, Indonesia
- Slums: India

### Employment

- Microfinancing: Bangladesh, Liberia, Iraq
- Entrepreneurial education: Uganda
- Mining cleanup: Chile
- Fruit trees: Kenya
- Farming: China, Mozambique, Egypt, Paraguay, Sri Lanka, Kenya, Java, Sudan
- Fertilizer: Ethiopia, Singapore, Cambodia, Bangladesh
- Drip irrigation: Israel, Senegal
- Rat traps: India
- Protecting livestock: Botswana, Central Asia, Namibia
- Dairy cooperatives: Afghanistan
- Restaurants: Cuba, Sierra Leone
- Crafts: China, Mozambique
- Crochet: Uganda
- Knitting: Bosnia, Kenya, Rwanda
- Sewing: Rio de Janeiro
- Rugs: Namibia, Afghanistan
- Beauticians: Afghanistan
- Eco-tourism: Peru
- Solar panel technicians: Bangladesh

## Global Projects Checklist, continued

### Health

➤ Dehydration: Rwanda
➤ Tuberculosis scanning: Mozambique, Tanzania
➤ Community kitchens: Peru
➤ Nutrition: Senegal, Sri Lanka, Nepal
➤ Stoves, solar cookers: Honduras, Philippines, Darfur, Bangladesh
➤ Personal hygiene: Mozambique
➤ Toilets: India

### Electricity, Fuel

➤ Light bulbs: Brazil, Philippines, Haiti
➤ Electricity: Bangladesh, Rwanda
➤ Mini-electric power plants: India
➤ Micro-hydropower: Indonesia
➤ Biogas: Bangladesh, Senegal, India, Kenya

### Water

➤ Emergency: Peru
➤ Wells: Africa
➤ Pumps: Sub-Sahara
➤ Filters: Dominican Republic, Kenya
➤ Water systems: Central America

### Transportation

➤ Safe transportation for women: India, Mexico, Lebanon
➤ Metrocable: Venezuela
➤ Traffic safety: Bolivia

### Environment

➤ Preserving forests: South America
➤ Preserving wildlife: Thailand, Africa, Cambodia, Panama, India, Indonesia, Madagascar

*As new projects are developed or additional needs are identified, the Global Projects checklist will naturally expand.*

The checklist can be a research tool for students that creates awareness of a variety of needs and solutions while helping them find specific solutions for specific challenges. Students would communicate with peers nationwide engaged in sister-city projects in similar geographical areas of the world, sharing problem-solving approaches, models, and outcomes. Over time, they would link to their global peers in this dialogue and become a global generation of problem solvers. The projects above would increase in number as we organize in this work.

Project originators in the global arena are current heroes in our world, our links to sustainable change in areas of great need. They are committed, long-term solution makers who pave a way that can be replicated or adapted. Their experience can help the education of our children. They can teach us to listen, to seek the input of others, to create lasting change that honors tribal custom or ethnic culture, and to support in sustainable ways. Our children, working with the guidance of project originators, can become a generation of heroes.

The beginning topics in the global checklist offer many projects that address reconciliation, healing, and shaping views toward peaceful and productive coexistence. These projects inform us that as humans—as adults—we don't have a track record for working together, living together, or solving problems together. We need to ask how we are addressing this issue in our children's education. We need to provide them with education that teaches them how to come together to create a world better than the one in which we live.

## Establishing a Dialogue

Experience with concepts of tolerance, diversity, and inclusion inform us we cannot assume what is best for another group of people from outside their daily living conditions, habits, customs, and history. We need to establish a dialogue and listen with genuine interest and respect to their perspective. Our children need to learn how to best start a relationship with their peers in a developing area of the world.

- What are the cultural norms and considerations that are involved?
- What are the environmental conditions?
- What is the starting point for communication?

Our children need to learn about current conditions and needs in the sister city:

- What beginning need is most meaningful to our sister city?
- How could a possible solution be sustained by the population of our sister city over time?

This information constitutes the preparation phase of the service learning structure that informs the action phase. I was introduced to a sister-city service learning project that drew upon these elements by Ken Sider, a third-grade teacher in our school district who introduced me to Ashok Mahaltra, a project originator and a professor at our local university.

## Our Sister City: The Ninash Foundation

Ashok was born in India. When his wife passed on early in her life, he promised her he would build schools for the poorest of the poor in India and has done so through the Ninash Foundation, which he created in honor of his wife. He makes regular trips to India and has created trustworthy, efficient, local partnerships essential to project success in places far away. He builds on outcomes and incorporates new initiatives that continue to evolve.

Ashok was our person "on the ground" who saw children picking up cow dung in the small village of Dundlod in northwest Rajasthan, India. These children were not permitted to attend school or drink from the same ladle with other children. He began to ask questions and seek solutions. Ashok sold a rental property in 1996 and used the proceeds to start the Ninash Foundation. The same year, in a one-room building donated by a local woman, 50 children began attending the first Indo-International School in Dundlod. The number of students attending grew to 150 by 1997. Another donated space accommodated this increase in students until the foundation gathered the funds necessary to build a school with six rooms in 2000. By 2006, the school included high school grades with science labs. As of 2012, the completed central school has twenty rooms and 550 children grades nursery through twelfth. After sixteen years, over a dozen of the school's girls have gone on to college. The school is now one of the best in the state and also includes economically and socially upper-class students.

Our city of Oneonta, New York, established a formal sister-city relationship with Dundlod in 2000. Our students learn about the other schools the Ninash Foundation has built, they learn about the results of sustained commitment that continue to build and grow new solutions, and they learn about solution-making role models. (www.ninash.org)

## Service Learning Outline:

As a service learning advocate, Ken Sider has experienced the increased student motivation and learning that results from student leadership roles in real-life contexts. Learning about the world and becoming an active participant are fundamental educational connects for him. Ken recognized the rich educational potential for his students if they were to learn about

India and the work of the Ninash Foundation, giving them an opportunity to find their places in the global world through the context of contribution.

In a K-12 service learning curriculum, students would get three years of experience with service learning leadership roles and projects by the time they reach third grade. Our students' global peers in developing areas of the world have of necessity often taken on adult responsibilities by the same age. With this perspective, youth on both sides of the equation are ready to have a conversation. Youth worldwide need connection with their peers—those who will be their peers as adults.

If our children take the lead, furthering the work of project originators, they will bring solutions to areas of need around the world and create relationships infused with appreciation and gratitude that grow among themselves as people who see human interactions in a different way than the previous generation does.

## Preparation

Once a sister city has been identified, students learn about the geography, climate, government, art, and culture of their sister city, and learning about genuine needs comes next. The need identified by our project originator was schools, but the starting point involved building relationships and trust.

Children in undeveloped areas of the world often engage in menial tasks to help their families survive. Releasing these children for school requires the sacrifice of this precious income, the sacrifice of a known value for an unknown, and to trust that change will occur as a result of education. Building this trust and creating a shift of perspective among families is the work of a project manager in the sister city. A critical part of our students' education is learning of this critical shift for families; they learn that relationship building comes before taking action, before the opportunity to affect long-lasting change.

Once families in our sister city met with Ashok and became invested in the idea of education and schools, the need was to identify a beginning location, however makeshift from our perspective, to provide teachers and basic supplies and then build schools.

Our students learn about the history of the Ninash Foundation; they learn that younger students began with writing on slate, which requires them to memorize as they learn, that their first activity of the day is yoga, and that students teach other children in their homes.

Building communication and relations among peers typically requires preparatory thought and discussion. In the beginning, because the children in Dundlod were learning three languages, Hindi, Rhajistani, and English, English was still difficult. If each of our students sent a letter, the principal at the school would have to translate them all. Someone suggested a composite letter from each class or a power point presentation as a better way to communicate—perhaps once a month—using pictures and a few words that were fairly self-explanatory and helpful in developing language. As education progressed in our sister city, traditional pen-pal relationships in English became possible.

Gathering children for education revealed the need for dietary support; proper nourishment of all students attending school was not secure. A kitchen added to the school in 2004 provided one nutritious meal for every child each day. Dairy goats became another solution: if each family got a goat, there would be an ongoing supply of milk, cheese, and yogurt for the poorest families of the children—families earning less than $1 a day. As the goats multiply, more opportunities for sustainable livelihood become possible.

Sending items or ourselves to areas far from home is not cost-effective. Cash converted into goods and services on the spot is most often the most practical way to help. In the preparation phase, students and teachers plan community events, fundraisers, and informational campaigns to generate these funds.

**Action**

Fundraisers that demonstrate learning are the best fit for service learning projects. In our school district, students create a public fundraiser where they sell Indian craft items they have made and perform Indian dances and songs. On average, with 25¢ sales, they raise $500.

If students learn about the art produced in their sister city, they can create items for sale such as bookmarks or stationery using indigenous techniques they have studied. If they learn about traditional foods from their sister city, they can try recipes and make recipe books for sale, create dishes for tastings, or contact restaurants to create these foods for a public event. If students learn about music and dance from their sister city, they can create a dance party around this theme as a fundraiser.

A high school student from London, who had visited the Indo-International School in Dundlod, created calendars combining children's art and life from Dundlod with children's art and life from London. All proceeds from the sale of the calendars fund field trips for the children of the Dundlod School.

Our students engaged in an interesting art project. Classes collected pennies while studying Rangoli, an Indian art form. Each class created an intricate Rangoli design on the cafeteria floor using pennies and invited all classes to the "Penny Art Rangoli Gallery." One such event yielded $450, which went to the Indo-International School in Dundlod to buy pencils and replenish the school's library.

Students learned about past project contributions and accomplishments as well as current needs. T-shirts made each year can list accomplishments to date, creating a fundraising activity that celebrates the effects of sustained community building and students' leadership roles in third grade.

Another example in our schools is the "Adopt-a-Goat" fundraiser, created to provide goats for our sister-city community members in need of a sustainable food source. If a class raises $60, its teacher kisses a goat at a celebration assembly, providing a fun incentive for this particular fundraising effort. The Ninash Foundation arranges for the purchase and distribution of goats in Dundlod.

Students and teachers who create new fundraising events based on learning about their sister city can add to an ever-evolving database of project components. Schools can submit successful ideas as well as draw on the work of others who have contributed to the database.

## Reflection

Opportunities for reflection abound in a sister-city relationship as students share contrasts between the cultures, as cooperative work takes place, and as friendships form. Although third graders manage the sister-city project, older grades can contribute, expanding opportunities for learning, giving, and reflection.

## Celebration

In an ongoing service learning project, everyone can share current and cumulative outcomes. Over the past six years, the fundraising efforts within our school district for the Adopt-A-Goat program have supported the donation of over 80 goats. Combined with donations from local residents in the sister city, the distribution of 200 goats has occurred.

Celebration can happen at many points in a sister-city project: a fundraiser that educates, a T-shirt that honors work to date, a news article about funds raised at an event, a school wall design that tracks fundraising outcomes, and a national database of many sister-city outcomes. With a service learning K-12 curriculum in place, sharing sister-city outcomes at a school assembly is a natural occurrence as one of many school-based service learning projects.

## Disciplines Incorporated

- Science
- Mathematics
- English Language Arts
- Social Studies
- Arts
- Career Development and Occupational Studies
- Languages other than English

Connecting students at home and abroad increases awareness of the role education plays not only in the life of the individual but also in the context of the world. When our children discover the life-changing significance education can bring to a family or community in a developing area and the level of sacrifice often required to attain it, they gain a fresh perspective on education in our country.

We need to develop our humanitarian outreach further, creating ever-deepening, constructive, peaceable connections with others worldwide. The sister-city component provides an ongoing, organized way for us to reach out in a sustained manner to developing areas of the world. If our youth come together worldwide to work productively for the best interest of all concerned, our view of what is possible will inevitably shift toward positive outcomes and hope for the future. If students maintain yearly communication, they could learn of the developing life goals of their sister-city peers and share perspectives on progress made at home and abroad. The concept of a nationwide graduating class would expand further to a global graduating class of young adults who have learned it is possible to work together based on their practical experience in making their world a better place; they will also have come to know a progression of solution-making that previous generations could not have envisioned.

## Fourth Grade: Disabilities Awareness

"Today, (July 2011) about 50 million Americans, or 1 in 5 people, are living with at least one disability, and most Americans will experience a disability some time during the course of their lives." (www.cdc.gov)

Addressing the variety of needs of community members challenged by disabilities requires community support beyond doctors and hospitals. Independent living centers (ILCs) provide skills training and resources to help people achieve self-determined living. Areas of support include adaptive technology, home modifications, independent living skills, personal care, transportation, education, and employment. Other integral considerations are networking, peer support, recreation, social interactions, and emotional support to combat isolation. ILCs work to educate and advocate for needed changes in society and to create a barrier-free society to support the greatest level of independence for all—an accessible community and equal rights in a context of unequal mobility.

Service learning approaches to the topic of disabilities often incorporate some form of simulation or experiential component to increase understanding of the dimension of challenge posed by a disability. Equally

51

important is real-life contact with people living with disabilities. From this combined perspective, accommodation, accessibility, and independence become more meaningful.

Ken Sider developed the Disabilities Awareness project in coordination with Don Wyckoff, the architectural barrier consultant for the Catskill Center for Independence. All students get the opportunity to spend a day in a wheelchair from the moment they arrive until the end of the school day, except for bathroom breaks. Students complete a contract outlining acceptable behavior, engage in a prewriting exercise identifying what they think they will experience, journal their experiences, invent something to address a specific challenge they faced, and finish with a final essay. Together, students create a documentary video to support their advocacy efforts. Their teacher also commits to a full day in a wheelchair.

## Materials

- Three nonmotorized, anti-tip wheelchairs: two small, one adult size (Most ILCs can lend wheelchairs. Wheelchair vendors will often donate wheelchairs for the cause directly to the schools or through nonprofit ILCs.)
- Digital/video camera
- Moviemaker program (optional)
- Tools for basic school on-site assessment:
  o tape measure
  o door pressure gauge
  o two-foot bubble level/accessibility stick

## Service Learning Outline:

## Preparation

A meeting with the ILC educator addresses the work of the organization, the range of disabilities, people-friendly language, and legislation concerning civil rights, discrimination, and accommodation. The ILC educator demonstrates how all parts of a wheelchair work: steering, locking, brakes, footrests, and traversing different ground surfaces and slopes.

In addition to providing a parental permission slip, students sign a behavior contract that requires respectful behavior, cooperative work with classmates, and requesting help only if they cannot complete a task by themselves. Students also complete a prewriting assignment on what they think the wheelchair experience will be like.

When it is their turn to spend a day in the wheelchair, students engage in a task list, attempting as possible, to:

- Go up and down the cafeteria ramp
- Pick up an object from the floor
- Open a classroom window
- Use a computer
- Wash their hands in the classroom sink
- Look in a mirror
- Find and sign out library books
- Hang up their coats and backpacks
- Take care of their own food at lunch
- With a partner and the teacher's permission, try exiting and entering the school's main door

Along with the task list, the following questionnaire lays the foundation for a personal essay assessing a variety of factors encountered in the wheelchair experience. Details, complete sentences, and parental support are advised.

- Were you comfortable in the wheelchair? How did your body feel?
- What was the most difficult thing you had to do while in the wheelchair?
- What tasks were impossible to do without help?
- How did you feel about asking for help?
- How did students (other than your classmates) treat you when you were in the wheelchair?
- Was there ever a moment when you wished to be out of the wheelchair? When? Why?
- When you went to specials (PE, music, etc.), how was it different?
- Was it easy or difficult to work at your desk? Why?
- Were you able to open doors? Was it difficult?
- Describe any challenges or frustrations you had at lunch.
- Describe any challenges or frustrations you had at recess.

- Did it take you longer to get things done while in the wheelchair? Share an example.
- If we had a disabled student with a wheelchair in our class, what changes should we make to our classroom?
- If you could build a better school, what changes would you make for disabled people?
- What have you learned from this experience?
- Have you changed the way you think about people in wheelchairs? If so, how?

The preparation phase creates awareness of environmental elements not designed or maintained to support the needs of people with disabilities. The concepts of "accessibility" and "accommodation" gain context and become meaningful terms that inspire advocacy for corrective action.

## Action

Using the Americans with Disabilities Acts Accessibility Guidelines for Buildings and Facilities (ADAAG) website, students determine on-site barriers to accessibility. Parking, exterior and interior paths of travel, ground surfaces, slopes and grades, level changes at doorways, door widths including latch-side clearance, door hardware, door pressure, door-pull force, hardware, table height, and reach height are assessed. Arm and hand strength, and dexterity are additional considerations. With this information, students create a report for school administrators on current conditions and solutions, noting violations of the Americans with Disabilities Act (ADA).

Students participate in documenting their experiences in the wheelchair with camera and video: two students are videographers each day, and two students are photographers each day. The photos and video footage become an educational video that supplements the students' presentation to school administration where they request answers for noncompliance.

Although only a few people carelessly park in the handicapped space, students noticed it and purchased an additional sign to place beneath the handicapped parking space, indicating "No student drop-off or pickup; NO deliveries." They also created "parking tickets" to remind violators.

## Reflection

Students describe and depict an idea for a helpful invention—an adaptive technology—based on their experience in the wheelchair. Their ideas included:

- Extensions to reach high places, pencil sharpeners, cabinets, etc.
- Umbrellas for rainy weather
- A robotic leg to kick a ball
- Four-wheel drive for hikes and walks
- A computer attached to a wheelchair
- Water bottle/cup holder
- Padding for arm rests
- Lunch tray carrier
- Table extension

For further reflection, students interacted with someone with a disability. Larry Qualtere, a local, shared with students his story of a swimming accident he had as a teen resulting in his need for a wheelchair and other adaptive technologies. He told them he could perform most activities, although it takes longer. He mentioned he needed to figure out ways to:

- Shower
- Brush his teeth
- Hold things
- Sign his name
- Eat sandwiches, pick up his glasses
- Drive
- Use a cell phone, camera, computer
- Play darts, video games, fish, hunt

Students were curious about the adaptive technologies Larry used to compensate for the paralysis in his fingers. He showed them:

- A special cup he can pick up
- A puff and sip mechanism that helps with different actions
- A red ball used with the back of his hand for the computer

55

He brought photos of items in his home:

- A lever on the door handle with a rope to pull the door closed
- A remote to lock and unlock the front door
- An electrical box with sixteen numbers so he can turn on lights, the fan, air conditioner, radio, and more

When Larry asked students for questions, they were well prepared for meaningful dialogue.

Student: "Are you comfortable in a wheelchair?"
Larry: "My back gets stiff. I have an air cushion in the chair that prevents sores."

Student: "Was it hard to open our school doors?"
Larry: "No. Doors are heavy. Eight pounds is the pressure for exterior doors. It often happens that I can't open doors. When I was visiting a friend, I got stuck in a small room for half an hour because it had only a door knob."

Student: "Do you have an upstairs?"
Larry: "Yes. I go out the first floor and up on the outside to a door to the upper floor."

Student: "Is it easy to drive?"
Larry: "Yes, but tricky!"

Student: "Have you met anyone else who is disabled?"
Larry: "Yes, I visit people who've just had accidents to give them hope and inspire them."

Larry also shared perspective he gained from living with a disability:

- Life is important.
- Be glad people look out for you.
- Be careful; think before you do things.
- Life can be hard for anyone; it's all about positive attitude.

- It's no fun to give up.
- Other people can give you ideas.

Students accompanied him to his van, which he entered independently via a ramp at the back of the van. He moved to the driver's seat and spoke with them from the window before leaving.

## Student Journal Excerpts

- "It looked like fun for all the kids, and I couldn't wait for my turn."
- "If I had to do it all the time, it wouldn't be fun. When you have to go fast, your arms hurt. Your legs hurt from not being able to move."
- "I watched my friends play in the snow and because I was in a wheelchair, I couldn't participate."
- "I felt so helpless. Even though I didn't want to bother anyone, I had to. I was embarrassed."
- "We shouldn't laugh at others—not just people in wheelchairs. It teaches you how to be nicer."
- "It helps with feelings."

Student essays excerpts:

- "If I could build a new school, I would add automatic doors everywhere. The doors are big, heavy, and difficult to open. I learned to be thankful for being able to walk. I never realized how hard it would be to get around in a wheelchair. I never really thought about people in wheelchairs before this, but I am aware of them now. Their disabilities are hard enough, yet they have so many challenges just getting around. I think we should do more to make our schools and towns easier for people with disabilities."

- "When I was going to the library, I noticed lots of kids staring at me. I saw a few of them giggling, too. I think they were laughing at me. I wished I could get out of the wheelchair and just walk to the library instead. During music, I had to park my wheelchair on the stage while everyone else sat on the steps. I felt all alone up there, and it was not much fun. I didn't feel like singing. I thought it would be easy to work at my desk, but I couldn't fit my legs and wheels under there. It was very frustrating. Thanks to my friends, I was able to get my cafeteria tray to the table. Without their help, I would have spilled my food on my lap. Sadly, I couldn't fit in at the table with my friends and had to eat on the end. It was a very difficult way to eat. Plus, everything took much longer to get done, even just finding things in my desk."

During the Disabilities Awareness project, students experience more than physical navigation challenges. When accessibility is not possible, they experience the lack of integration and inclusion—the inability to participate that creates social isolation. These experiences motivate and inform their advocacy work. Students learn about the processes and skills that combine to create change in their world. Encounters with people who are meeting the challenges of living with disabilities can additionally inspire them to believe in their capabilities to meet their own challenges.

## Celebration

All student essays get published in a special commemorative book. Sharing the project at an assembly allows younger students to anticipate and older students to reflect on their encounters with disability.

Our local ILC offered a pizza party to thank the students for their work. The students chose instead to put the money that would have been spent on the party into an account that would be used for future accessibility projects. The ILC also donated an item the students had identified in their project work: an accessible doorbell for the main entrance to the school.

## Project Outcomes

- New accessible playground equipment
- Accessible cafeteria tables
- Improved signage
- Doorbell for those who cannot open the front door
- Annual remediation of violations of the ADAAG (assessed by students)

- Growing awareness of disability etiquette and advocacy evidenced in the school culture
- Campaign by students to spread awareness throughout central New York via posters, billboards, and radio spots in coordination with the County Office of Emergency Services and the local ILC
- Two college education majors adopted the project at our local university, compiling photos and data on the condition of the "accessible campus." Their presentation for deans, professors, and assorted staff produced great response and prompted repairs around campus. Since then, these students have presented the project and outcomes twice a year to other education majors.
- The project has been adopted by schools in Alaska, New Jersey, Pennsylvania, Rhode Island, and Texas, affecting approximately 1,500 students.

## Disciplines Incorporated

- English Language Arts
- Mathematics, Science, and Technology
- Social Studies
- Career Development and Occupational Studies
- Health, Physical Education, and Home Economics
- Arts

## Responses

From teachers:

- "We can talk and read about it, but nothing can replace the experience."
- "The project is becoming part of the culture of the school."

From a parent:

- "We honor the handicapped by providing "handicapped access" and support services, but this project develops heightened awareness and sensitivity at a much deeper level."

From a person with a disability:

- "I think it's good for students to be more aware of problems facing people with disabilities. The world in a wheelchair is a very difficult place. There are a lot of laws helping the disabled, but until you have to deal with that world, you don't know how inaccessible things can be."

From ILC staff:

- "This project promotes tolerance and understanding. It significantly plants the seed of tolerance."
- "The project is an excellent opportunity to show students what it's like to have a disability. When members of the organization come to talk about the Americans with Disabilities Act, it will make sense to them now that they have seen the barriers."
- "Elementary school is the best time to instill awareness of disabilities; it creates a lasting impression."
- "I think this is really a great project, and I would so love to see it make its way around to all the schools in the nation as a whole!"
- "Educating the students through this experience will accomplish more in the way of a totally inclusive, accessible environment than any bill or law has ever had the power to do. The experience is sure to change anyone who participates in it. Turning sympathy into empathy is the key to move our next generation of lawmakers, code enforcers, business owners and even homeowners who will have the foresight to make their homes accessible long before they may ever need it to be."

## Expansion

Local ILC staff identified a significant need: to boost the employment rate of young adults with disabilities in our community. The framework for a possible middle school service learning project to address this need follows.

## Preparation

Staff from our ILC talk with students about the current high unemployment rate after graduation for those with disabilities in our community; students learn that the ILC needs support to help students with disabilities prepare during high school for the transition to employment.

## Action

The suggestion of the ILC staff member was to create lifelines of people with disabilities who are or were successfully employed and how they achieved this. Inspirational quotes could be included. The purpose is to provide inspiring examples to students with disabilities in middle school and help them identify employment goals and structure their studies through high school to achieve their goal. This provides sufficient time to develop skills and to give focus to their work leading to graduation.

Our ILC educator could help identify successfully employed individuals with disabilities from the community for middle school students to interview. If this project were part of the K-12 service learning model, students nationwide could add local research to a national pool of information. This larger body of examples could then be broken down by specific disabilities. The local ILC educator could then direct students to gather examples of specific disabilities based on current needs in the community each year, thereby increasing relevancy.

## Reflection

Student reflections on this project would build on their reflections in the Disabilities Awareness program.

## Celebration

Student-created lifelines could be posted on a bulletin board and, afterward, be given to the special education department for ongoing use. A school-wide assembly, perhaps during Disabilities Awareness Month, would provide opportunity to honor those interviewed, supporting the integration of people with disabilities into the larger community. In an ongoing service learning curriculum, students with disabilities could look forward to be honored as they work toward successful employment after graduation.

Other projects under the topic of disabilities in my database explore blindness, deafness, and physical conditions related to aging that require problem solving and adaptation. There are models for buddy relationships based on tutoring, assistance with living and work-related skills, and physical education. Certain projects foster inclusion in activities such as cheerleading, proms, and programs in music and dance that draw out creative expression.

# Fifth Grade: Food2Share

Food2Share was originally conceived as a district-wide model since food could be garnered from all school cafeterias. This creates opportunity for daily involvement for all students at all grade levels. The initial setup for the program can be based on information outlined in part one.

When Food2Share was up and running in our schools, a fifth-grade teacher asked for the donation statistics from our food bank for use in a graphing unit for her students. Another fifth-grade teacher suggested that her class could make regular updates to a Food2Share graph and post it in the cafeteria. Fifth grade seemed the logical elementary grade to take the leadership role for Food2Share: teachers identified a curricular connection, students would have participated in the program since kindergarten, and there was not yet a leadership service learning role for fifth grade.

### Service Learning Outline:

### Preparation

As fifth graders take on this new leadership role, they learn more about the history of the project and support materials that make the project viable. They meet with the director of a food bank to discuss the project and learn more about the work of the food bank and food insecurity in their community.

## Action

Fifth graders create graphs that incorporate current information from the food bank and previous statistics graphed by former fifth graders.

## Reflection

Prior to this leadership role, students have participated in the program and heard their peers and food bank staffers describe the project in assemblies. Such student involvement over a period of years allows for reflection in greater depth on food insecurity—how it relates to the overall health of their communities, how it has intersected with their lives, and how it affects their sister city.

## Celebration

Project outcomes are updated and shared publicly each month in graphs that track donations to date. Yearly assemblies further celebrate project success and address ongoing goals.

## Disciplines Incorporated

- Mathematics
- Language Arts
- Health

## Expansion

Project topics from schools in my database include:

- Early-age whole foods exploration
- Gardening
- School markets
- Garden harvested food products
- Cooking
- Salad bars
- Family-style dining

- Weekend backpacks
- Summer lunches

Community involvements include:

- Gardening
- Field gleaning
- Restaurant donations
- Grocery store donations
- Mobile meals
- Pay-what-you-can restaurants
- Urban fish farming

# Sixth Grade: Recycling and Zero Waste

We face many environmental challenges, and while some areas of problem solving may still involve debate regarding best solutions, other areas, such as recycling, are more straightforward. Although many of us are demonstrating progressive awareness that a piece of trash may require assessment to determine its category and destination, we have to make much more progress.

In most communities and homes, recycling tends to focus on a few categories of waste, such as paper, glass, and plastic. The complete elimination of waste in concept and in practice requires much more planning and thought. The Zero Waste Alliance provided the following visual aids on its website to contrast our current efforts with the attainable goal of zero waste. (www.zerowaste.org)

## Material Flows Today

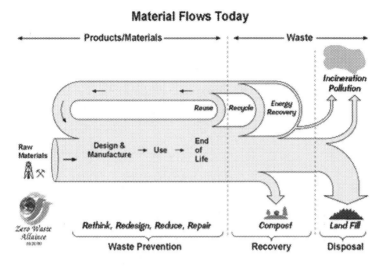

## Improved Material Flows

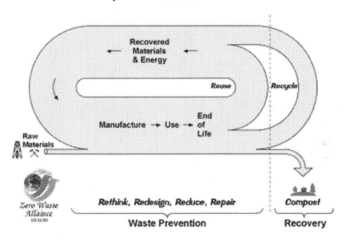

If we gather progressive models, we can begin to address the issue of waste in a more comprehensive manner. If we bring these models to our schools and the education of our youth, the greatest influx of change will occur as they bring awareness and improved habits to their homes and communities. We can create a K-12 service learning community leadership role for recycling, managed and tracked by sixth graders, that educates and promotes lifelong habits of recycling, which will strengthen progressive care for the environment among us all.

## Programs in Schools

Many schools have already begun significant work in addressing school waste with their students. A common starting point in schools is analyzing existing waste by collecting, weighing, and examining a day's worth of garbage, which creates a base line from which to monitor progress over time. Students identify categories of waste and seek ways to recycle and reduce waste. Once they determine a course of action, they get the supplies they need and inform the school community of the new systems and processes.

Students have created skits to teach recycling information to their peers, infomercials on waste-free lunches, environmental rap songs, posters, and bulletin boards with reminders and tips. As students track their progress, their daily contributions accrue to contrast with their beginning waste data. The significance of these results would compound if schools tracked their progress in a common database.

Students who bring lunch from home can make it waste-free by using reusable lunch bags and containers. Foods such as apples, oranges, and bananas become healthier alternatives to packaged snacks. Cafeteria food service in schools pursuing reduced waste may opt for flatware instead of plastic utensils, family-style dining and/or compostable salad bowls. Students dump any leftover milk and place their cartons in a recycling bin.

Organics become a separate waste stream. Some schools send organic waste to composting facilities or farmers for composting or feed for pigs, creating significant reduction in hauling costs. Other schools take advantage of the educational opportunity provided by vermiculture—worm composting. Students in these schools become involved with classroom worm bins, creating compost for school gardens or for sale. Food service may join in with composters in school kitchens, adding to the supply of compost for school gardens.

Digging deeper into the cycle, some students in our country have school gardens in which they raise food for their cafeterias. Students who engage in this full cycle of growing and tasting their own food become more sensitive to the amount of effort it takes to grow it. The administrators of such programs typically find them to be cost effective, as produce is sold to the school. The bridge to environmental science is strengthened in schools that have teaching gardens, green roofs, and rain barrels to recycle water.

Although the emphasis of this writing is on a K-12 curriculum, our college and university communities increase our store of models. Universities and colleges in Illinois, Vermont, and California have either herds of cows producing all their milk, yogurt, and sour cream, their own hens for cage-free eggs, their own apple orchards, or their facilities management vehicles running on dining-hall cooking oil. These advanced-learning environments continue to design progressive models for our communities.

All these examples from our schools represent pieces of what could become a collective, comprehensive model disseminated nationally for work in all K-12 schools, bringing the best of all solutions together for all our youth and our communities. Programs often pay for themselves, and hauling costs can go down. Even more far-reaching are the benefits of experiential learning and instilling progressive habits among our youth—the influx of health as our children get more-natural produce and new foods to explore because of their labors and education. Overall morale typically increases among staff, teachers, and students with the adoption of these community-building programs. The schools in my database with the components above are in California, Colorado, Illinois, Maine, Maryland, Missouri, New Jersey, New York, Ohio, Vermont, and Ontario.

## Programs in Communities

Model community programs have developed in a variety of locations nationwide. If we were to bring these models to the national checklist of projects, to the attention of our children, and to the attention of our community members, we could gradually adopt and create processes for recycling different categories of waste, with the support of others who have already done so. Community members and committees could turn to a national list of projects to learn how others have solved a particular problem rather than wasting time or momentum wondering how others have done so. The optimum goal for all, over time, would be zero waste.

There are several approaches to assessing waste streams. When we have an item that we categorize as trash, we can check it against the national checklist to see how others are recycling it. We can assess community businesses by type, using model programs for specific businesses. We can assess products we purchase to determine the complete life cycle of the product in relation to the concept of zero waste.

States from my collection with components to contribute are California, Florida, Georgia, Illinois, Indiana, Maine, Massachusetts, Michigan, Minnesota, New Jersey, New York, Ohio, Oregon, Pennsylvania, Vermont, Virginia, Washington, and Wisconsin.

## Item by Item

Textiles are one category of waste. Beyond reuse as second-hand clothing, textile discards can be converted into fiber for use in new textile products or for wiping and polishing cloths.

Worn-out sneakers can be ground up to make sports surfaces. Scrap tires are becoming fill material in road and building projects, for playground pads, and tire-derived fuel.

Building materials are another category. Deconstruction models call for reusable material from demolition sites or homes under construction to go to construction-supply recycling organizations where contractors and others buy them. Homeowners and private contractors can also donate to these organizations. Construction and demolition recyclers handle items such as wood, brick, concrete, roofing shingles, and metal. Wood not suitable for reuse can be cut into firewood and kindling.

Composting organics—food scraps and food-soiled paper—creates a valuable resource that can go into landscaping and construction projects to replenish soil, reduce erosion, prevent storm water runoff from contaminating wetlands, lakes, and streams, and capture carbon dioxide for climate protection. Specific organic items for composting include:

- Food scraps: fruits and vegetables, meat, fish, and bones, bread, other baked goods, pasta, egg shells, dairy products, and coffee grounds
- Food-soiled paper products: paper towels and napkins, paper plates and cups, milk and juice cartons, pizza boxes, egg cartons, boxes from frozen and refrigerated foods, waxed paper and paper containers, coffee filters and tea bags
- Other items: full vacuum cleaner bags, dryer lint, tissues and cotton balls, floral trimmings and house plants

Different collection models abound in our communities. Waste haulers may provide organics carts for pickup every week on trash day.

Some communities sell backyard composters, and others subsidize the cost of home composters. Some communities include yard debris with compost collection; others separate these two categories of compostable material. Cities may own a compost site that sells compost and mulch. Yard debris can be collected year-round or seasonally. One community collects fall leaves curbside, mulches them, and delivers the mulch to residents free of charge.

Some cities have over twenty categories of "waste" for recycling. Some models have drop-off stations; some pick up over twenty categories of recyclable materials weekly. Some sort glass by color to save the cost of an intermediate processor; others have online guides with search options for instructions and information on recycling specific items.

"Discard malls" allow businesses that recycle and consumers to drop off unwanted items. Some have an area of a recycling center where reusable items such as furniture, books, and clothing are available for free to residents. Some cities have for-profit centers that include repair and refurbishment of items for sale. There is even a recycling incentive program to stimulate more recycling: recyclables get weighed on pickup, and based on the weight, those bringing the recyclables get reward dollars good at stores and earth-friendly product discounts.

There are communities that recycle:

- organics
- milk, juice, and drink cartons
- cereal boxes
- aluminum trays and foils
- steel and aluminum cans
- plastic bottles: #1,2,3
- glass sorted by color
- metal clothing hangers
- mattresses and box springs
- textiles
- cork
- batteries
- auto and button batteries
- fluorescent bulbs
- paint
- tires
- used motor oil

- scrap metal
- construction materials, fixtures
- concrete and asphalt

With a list of specific categories or items that communities are recycling nationwide, we can check off the things recycled in our own communities and seek models from others for the things we do not currently recycle. With a checklist managed in our schools, we would not need to educate our children about recycling, as they would be partners in promoting improvements and managing information regarding recycling in their communities.

## Business by Business

Businesses generate different kinds of waste based on their products and activities. Models from businesses engaged in exemplary recycling programs can support us in bringing solutions to our community businesses.

Some food service models compost 100 percent of food discards from kitchen and dining rooms. Rendering companies pick up meat products and kitchen grease. There are models for hospitals, shopping malls, fairgrounds, and festivals. Some correctional centers turn mattress cotton into a compost bulking agent. Some grocery stores take old flowers and greens from floral departments, waxed cardboard, preconsumer scraps from in-store cafes, wilted and spoiled produce, and corrugated cardboard for composting. In one grocery store model, organics that include spoils, out-of-date bakery, dairy, and deli items, old seafood, soiled paper products, and food spills go into waxed cardboard boxes and get compacted. A hauling company takes the compacted organics to a composting site where they are ground with yard trimmings and composted. The nutrient-rich finished compost is screened to remove contaminants and sold to farmers, golf courses, and land reclamation projects.

This information can raise awareness in our schools and beyond. As we build a K-12 service learning model, the parents and relatives of our children become involved—they are doctors, nurses, grocery store managers, business owners and their staff, and extended family members.

When we know how specific businesses are accomplishing replication-worthy results, we can suggest solutions or components of models along with contacts for additional support. With a checklist managed by schools, the trickle-down effect into our communities could happen in a number of ways. For example, some doctors' offices and hospitals recycle outdated X-ray film. Maybe doctors, nurses, or hospital staff members take their children to school and look for model practices under hospitals on the national checklist of projects. They could take a question to their staff or inform the school that their workplace does in fact recycle such film, and sixth graders could update this information on the community checklist.

A checklist prompts us to ask and not assume as we update our community information. Students and others might ask their dentists if they recycle X-rays. If not, they can connect the dentists with organizations that do so. People could then read a list of dentists who are recycling and notice theirs is not on it. A simple phone call can help students update community information.

We should applaud the efforts of our hospitals, doctors, and dentists who are recycling. With models and resources that instruct, we are better able to make changes and take collective pride in the progress we make.

As our youth interact with businesses, they will learn best practices that will influence their choices in the variety of occupations they will hold as adults and bring wonderfully improved habits to the workplace. A nationwide education model secures the integration of these habits among all of us.

## Product by Product

As we develop the habit of recycling and considering waste as resource, we will consider the waste-stream outcomes of the products we buy. Instead of waiting until an item is no longer functioning to wonder how we can dispose of it, we can begin at the beginning—before we even buy it. Many times I have found myself with questions about replacement parts or ingredients when shopping and used my cell phone to call the company—either in an aisle as I assess a product or in the grocery store line. This immediate feedback to companies helps inform their decision making for the manufacture of their products. What is important to consumers is important to manufacturers.

As our youth grow in understanding and working with the zero-waste concept, they can better consider the design of the entire life cycle of a product: can it be reused, recycled, or composted easily when the user finishes with it? Our youth will come to see that waste is actually bad design—the result of bad decision making. As they assess the full life cycle of products, they may begin to question whether they really need a product. As chemical waste comes to their attention as an element of our waste stream, they may search to discover the role toxics play in production. Shipping distance and packaging become further considerations.

End-of-life industry responsibility for products and packaging is an important objective in achieving the goal of zero waste. We can grow a generation of adults who are so well versed in the basics and habits of recycling and goals of zero waste that they demand the cooperation of businesses and manufacturers. These young people will eventually populate our management positions and bring greater awareness from an educational foundation that embraced many service learning leadership roles and contexts in their communities and sister-city relations. Our youth will gradually unite worldwide to address a multitude of overlapping issues that will inform their decision making at the personal and local level, with awareness of the refractions of their actions at the national and global level.

Our youth may become advocates who help curb excessive consumerism and encourage their parents to purchase, as financially possible, more-durable and repairable products. Our youth will ask questions that we may not be able to answer; they will not be satisfied with complaints or explaining why problems exist. They will seek solutions or solution makers and take action; they will want to do better together as a generation that rises above the performance of past generations. They will seek solutions as a direct result of their educational involvements in their communities. Expectations and inspiration will rise as solutions become tangible.

In such an evolving context, companies may respond more quickly to a changing market with modular designs to upgrade complex products or by leasing some products with full-service guarantees instead of selling them outright; responsible usage replaces ownership. Youth with comprehensive service learning experience will gradually enter fields of product design and manufacture. They will notice improvements they can make, be mindful of long-term solutions and planning, and incorporate environmental stewardship. Their scope and interests—their goals—will be larger than the realm of company profits.

As our youth organize and handle community information against a backdrop of nationwide models of excellence, they will take pride in their roles and contributions; they will see progress in which they have been involved and evidence of their work in the community and nationwide. Our children will become communicators, information seekers, and disseminators. If they get the opportunity to work with us as they grow, they will continue to work with us. If they are involved in constructive work with their peers as children, they will continue in constructive work with their peers as adults.

# Grades Seven through Twelve

With an experiential leadership component threaded constructively throughout the grade school experience, students who enter middle school will be decidedly different. They will bring an authentic desire for education that continues to include opportunities to use their knowledge and abilities in ways of value to others. Having a track record of making a difference and a national checklist of projects, our students will be able to make decisions about their next projects. Teachers can opt for projects that reflect content alignment with their specific disciplines.

Students emerging from this grade school foundation of service learning will have communicated with their peers nationwide and globally and seen the outcomes of their combined efforts. They will have seen solutions begin to form in developing areas of the world and the markings of peaceable, productive relationships evolving from nationwide outreach. They will know that younger students sustain and develop the leadership grade school projects in which they engaged.

The goal as we build through these middle and high school years will be to maintain continuity, providing progressive layers of service leadership work for our emerging young adults.

## Food2Share Expansion

Information from our food banks and models from the database along with work done by students in my college classes suggested the following layers of expansion:

- Grades 7, 8: global food donations
- Grades 9, 10: grocery store donations
- Grades 11, 12: restaurant donations

## Grades 7-8: Global Food Donations

Freerice.com is a website that utilizes multiple-choice exercises to strengthen a variety of academic subjects. Rice is donated to developing nations through the United Nations World Food Program (WFP) based on correct answers.

## Possible Service Learning Outline:

## Preparation

Visit poverty.com for class discussion.

## Action

Visit www.thehungersite.com to donate a cup of food to an impoverished person. Then go to www.freerice.com to engage in progressive skill building in areas such as English vocabulary and grammar, humanities (famous paintings and literature), chemistry, human anatomy, geography (flags of the world, countries, world capitals, landmarks), math (multiplication table and prealgebra), languages (German, Spanish, French, Italian), and SAT preparation. Success in these skill-building areas generates rice to support the global need for food.

## Reflection

Write a personal reflection on global food insecurity, drawing on sister-city information and community efforts to address local food insecurity.

## Celebration

Total rice donations and scores in academic areas on freerice.com can be shared in a school-wide assembly and with the community. The inclusion of statewide and national outcomes could expand recognition that we are a powerful force for good when we work together. Fifth graders would add these global food donations statistics to a graph that represents total food donations from the community.

## Middle School Language Arts Teacher Perspective:

- "Students are driven by the positive reinforcement of rice given. The beauty of it is that it hits every level. I have kids who have poor language skills, yet the levels on freerice.com meet their need. Students can chart their progress in the vocabulary levels. Students were very excited to play the game knowing they were increasing their language skills and helping people around the world."

## Grades 9/10: Grocery Store Donations

Dialogue with food bank staff can reveal a need for specific food items. The food bank may be in need of tuna fish or peanut butter but receive donations of pasta and baked goods. While all donations are appreciated, needed items may be difficult to obtain. One of our faith-based food pantry staff provided this perspective: "I ask for specific items in the church bulletin but we don't receive them. We have lots of spaghetti, but people still bring spaghetti because they always bring spaghetti."

In a grocery store food-garnering service learning model, students get a specific shopping list from the food bank and create a check-off list of needed items that can be displayed at the grocery store entrance. Community members would check off their donations to reflect new quantities needed. Information about how food insecurity is being met, along with the fifth-grade graph, would be posted in this location. The grocery store could donate any frozen or dairy items reaching their due date, thereby reducing organic waste and hauling costs for the store.

Students transport all donated items to the food bank each week and stock the shelves. They would also organize volunteer support to maintain the project during vacations.

## Grades 11/12: Restaurant Donations

Certain restaurants and food service companies regularly donate excess food to food banks. Older students can develop communication and presentation skills through advocacy work with community restaurants to bring them onboard with this natural opportunity to give back. Restaurants already engaged in excess food donation can help other restaurant owners see how some in the industry are accomplishing this much-needed community contribution. Students would share information with restaurant owners to create more ongoing partnerships between local restaurants and food banks.

Volunteer transport is the other project component students could coordinate. Local businesspeople or restaurant employees often find this volunteer transport role adds a valuable and convenient service component to their lives as they can drop off food at the food bank on their way home from work. Students could create and maintain volunteer support information.

City Harvest of New York City has a "street fleet" of corporate volunteers who help capture the small amounts of food that would not be cost-effective to pick up with larger trucks. Our students could learn, through a national checklist of projects, of communities managing transport challenges along with setup specifics. In a nationwide K-12 curriculum, over time, everyone would become familiar with these programs and how they work.

As grocery stores and restaurants get on track to donate excess food, their donations are acknowledged in updates from the food bank and represented in fifth graders' graphs.

## Tax Credit: A Hidden Detail of Support

When the food bank began sending donation statistics, they also included a dollar amount for tax credit. The director of the food bank explained that there could be tax credit for donations from for-profit restaurants and food service companies. A fuller cycle of giving thus presented itself: what if the for-profit food service in our public schools had given leftover frozen foods? They could have received a tax credit, the dollar amount of which could have been donated to our youth for more service work.

What a wonderful cycle among us all, with the added benefit of free marketing for the food service not only to parents but also to the next generation of adults coming to know of their good work in giving back to the community. It would cost them nothing. The realization of this fragment of potential would provide students with some extra funds for use in their service projects. Restaurants and grocery stores that donate excess food could also pass these tax savings on as donations to youth actively involved in bettering their communities.

# A K-12 Service Learning Journal

Reflection is one of the four components of service learning. A K-12 service learning curriculum that spanned multiple needs and approaches to community problem solving could include an ongoing journaling component sustained from kindergarten through graduation. Reflections could be stimulated from a variety of perspectives, creating a record of contributions to local, national, and global needs throughout the entire K-12 education. Students could draw comparisons and discover overlaps, commonalities, and distinctions between the different areas of community service work in which they have engaged.

These journals would capture all service components in one document that students take with them upon graduation, providing evidence they were able to take actions that bettered their world. It would show that they always had a place in their communities, their country, and the world and that they took responsibility for something beyond themselves in partnership with their local, national, and global peers.

A K-12 journal becomes a piece of personal and community history, a history of growth in leadership, a history of progress in different areas of problem solving, a history that coincides with their nationwide graduating class, and a history that overlaps with their peers in surrounding grades. The journal is a way to remember and share stories and differences with future generations of youth who can see the foundation they laid or upon which they continue to build.

# PART THREE

▼

# "For the People"

There are many in need in our neighborhoods, across the country, and around the world. When we help others, we also help ourselves by creating a better and safer world for all of us. Thus, "for the people" becomes an all-inclusive worldwide concept.

## SUSTAINABILITY

The outcomes of a K-12 service learning model spread nationwide with a sister-city component would truly be for the people, for us all. When we consider the magnitude of solutions a K-12 service learning model could bring to our world—the way in which outcomes would circle back to our families, to our children, to the environment, to future generations—it becomes an all-encompassing idea. The need to "do it right" becomes essential, and how to properly care for an idea so rich with potential becomes a critical consideration. What kind of structure is needed? Who should be in charge? Whom could we trust? How do we protect and sustain it generation to generation?

A K-12 national service learning curriculum would create an overarching sustainable structure with our youth watching over our world; a structure within our schools—easily identifiable locations—constantly refreshed with new life and energy to solve new challenges and maintain ongoing projects.

Placing the management of a community checklist of projects in our schools ensures sustainability. When an organization or individual leaves a project, another can pick it up where a vacancy shows on the checklist of projects. As community members engage in projects on a community checklist, a reserve of people accrues who can provide additional information and support as responsibility for projects shifts.

Without a larger sustaining framework, service projects eventually fall into the vacuum of lost projects—as teachers retire, as new principals take over, as new agendas arise, as interests shift. Community-based organizations know from experience that support can dry up at any time. They live, like their clients, on the edge. Year after year they muster the energy to "raise community awareness," knowing that they will need to repeat these efforts to reawaken community members. Their work and the daily progression of needs they address continue, while we, for the most part, forget as we focus on personal responsibilities.

In our community, in spite of the wonderful outcomes created by Food2Share, the project gradually dwindled over several years. As my inspiration grew for the larger idea of a K-12 service learning model, I came to find, as have many others, that projects currently don't survive without a single individual to drive individual projects. Although projects were created at different grade levels, without an overarching structure of support, they gradually disappeared. We have the ability, the resources, and the will to contribute, to volunteer, and to effect change, but our efforts fluctuate without a structure to inform and sustain our giving.

Sustainability has become a critical assessment factor for many initiatives. The qualities that create sustained outcomes are many, and although familiar, their combination is daunting and complex: long-term planning and vision, ownership, commitment, responsibility, dependability, motivation, persistence, flexibility, cooperation, trust, patience, maintenance, consistency, routines, ongoing education and assessment, contribution, and often sacrifice. When we assess sustainability from the vantage point of these qualities, it becomes easier to understand why it is difficult to achieve.

Sustaining an idea or endeavor is demanding work. Although we are capable of expressing the above qualities, overall we do not do so with consistency. Yet, regardless of how far we stray from the above qualities, we continue to strive toward the high demand of sustainability, an ideal that exceeds our essential human condition. Project originators are a group among us who demonstrate the blend of necessary qualities to achieve sustained outcomes.

# Project Originators

Service project originators are eager to share their work. Instead of personal gain, they seek solutions for environmental and human needs. They find satisfaction in progressive work toward goals beyond the self. They teach us how to come together and build community, serving as role models in many ways. When I worked with a project originator to expand a service learning project he had created into a district-wide model, this was his response:

> Though I may be considered the district's leader, this year I feel like one member of a team. That's a new experience—and a nice one. I am willing to meet with or present to anyone or any group. If there is a niche I can fill, let me know. This program is a good one. I think the combined momentum could keep it going for a long time. It's nice to be on a team. Thanks for making it happen.

This response is typical for project originators. There is no blockage to sharing and creating—they seek expansion of the good outcomes they have created. They take responsibility, have excellent follow-through, don't give up, continue to care for those with whom they have created relationships, and seek to include others in common endeavors. They welcome diversity of contributions, care for others, and play well with others in highly constructive ways.

So often we speak of learning from history—learning from our mistakes. How invigorating would it be to focus on learning from current solution-builders, to shift our focus toward positive, progressive expectations? Project originators see problems, but more important, they see solutions. They refer to problems, but they talk about solutions and seek others to join them in creating them. They need others to work with them and follow their lead. They seek to educate and bring more of us into their problem-solving arena. They show us the feasibility of significant and inspiring change. They show us the way forward. A K-12 service learning curriculum would honor their work, bringing much needed support as they continue to carve the way forward with our children as partners.

# SCHOOLS AT THE CENTER OF OUR COMMUNITIES

Schools are a large, central, and stable entity in all communities and provide a unifying, preexisting structure with mission values that embrace civic engagement. They are also the most powerful, central location for managing checklists of projects through which our civic activities can circulate. Schools naturally provide the vehicle for widespread communication within and between communities nationwide as well as globally—everyone easily gets on the same page. Our children and their educators can learn the best current practices along with the identification of new needs and solutions through school assemblies; this will allow them to continue expanding the model and unite us nationwide as Americans.

Placing our children at the center of managing community needs and solutions honors their education and capacity for contribution. Through real-life engagements and active participation with us, our children find relevance in their education and purposeful connections in their communities. Students see how their work fits into a larger national or global perspective and come to understand needs, but more important, to generate solutions. They experience the value of organization, contribution, and ongoing assessment of community needs as they join with their peers nationwide to share in solutions and outcomes.

Students also find value in their presence in the community when organizations come to them with needs and when community members come to them for information or with donations or to offer to volunteer.

Teachers experience increased student motivation and engagement in the classroom and find multiple leadership and learning experiences provided by the initiative. They get inspiration from the impact of their work with students in the community, and they become able to share in common work and outcomes with teachers nationwide, broadening their contributions to society.

Parents find channels of community service engagement with their children throughout the K-12 experience. They become educated about solutions for community needs through their children, who eventually become adults educated in this way, bringing further support to the next generation's contributions.

Community members have a central location for a well-organized overview of community needs and how they can be met. The impact of their contributions deepens as it passes through the awareness—the hands, hearts, and minds—of our youth. Community members find tangible evidence of the ability of the next generation to make a difference in the world, and this can create intergenerational bonds, with the next generation at the helm.

When businesses have access to a community checklist of projects, they find opportunities to give back to the community. What better way for businesses to market themselves than through giving back, coming directly to schools to see how they can contribute instead of waiting for solicitations for help. Interaction with businesses in this context expands real-world interactions for students and offers best practices to the next generation.

Community-based organizations benefit from a central informational location that creates ongoing awareness of needs. A central location provides them with a way to communicate needs, coordinate pickup of supplies or funds, share volunteer needs, and educate the community about the work of their organizations. Community-based organizations would also be able to find solutions from other parts of the United States and be uplifted by the flow of ongoing, dependable support.

With schools at the center of our communities, community members encounter verifiable evidence that our children are learning and becoming capable, contributing citizens. Youth are stimulated to learn by doing real-world work. Adults are inspired to consider the overall health of their communities and how they can contribute as they become directly involved with the learning of youth in their communities.

## The Curriculum

Service learning embraces a high level of flexibility and adapts to changes. Service projects reflect the conditions of our lives, our communities, and our world. Today's challenges may not be those of tomorrow, and that which needs research today may need maintenance tomorrow.

Our children encounter real-world change with service learning. Solutions may come from unexpected sources that require revamping original plans. Our children learn cooperatively, facing and managing challenge, failure, success, and growth together. The entire process teaches them much about life, problem solving, and how to travel rough or unknown paths. The learning that takes place in this safe, inclusive environment is transferable knowledge that supports success in more-traditional, individually assessed academic settings.

The structural underpinnings of this curriculum include the four-part design of service learning, signature grade-level service learning projects, and a national checklist of projects organized by topics as a resource for locally defined community checklists. Evaluation comes from statistical data generated by community-based organizations that offers tangible evidence of our efforts.

Curriculum for other core subjects (math, history, science, language arts) is determined by each state, reflecting the high value we place on freedom and autonomy. The service learning curriculum, by contrast, is nationally coordinated, reflecting the voice of the people to self-govern from a different perspective. A flexible service learning curriculum provides another avenue of expression for our core American value of freedom of voice and freedom to self-determine our path and how to get there.

A service learning curriculum invites the participation of all who discover better ways of meeting local, national, and global needs, "the people"—our youth, our teachers, and our community members—who bring problems to light and solutions to a collective table. Such a combined effort gathers our youth together with us on a journey worth pursuing, a journey that inspires us to continue.

## Simple Entry Models

A national model for service learning must be based on easily replicated projects with clear and valuable outcomes. Simple, core projects at specific grade levels create a foundation on which more-complex projects can develop.

The early-grade service learning projects for the K-12 model shared in previous chapters were created with teachers who were not initially familiar with service learning as an educational structure. However, with some explanation of service learning as a way to tie service to curriculum, they readily engaged. The practical, educational relevance of the service learning projects became clear to students, teachers, parents, community members, and elected officials as community-based organizations substantiated outcomes that confirmed the significance of contributions.

Simple models with clear explanations and support materials help teachers and students move forward into projects with greater ease and communication. Sample model formats are at www. k12serviceinitiative.com.

A dear friend, whose professional work involved event planning, once remarked that recurring events were "cookbook"—they had become as easy as a recipe. Once these grade-level projects are up and running, less energy is required to maintain them because habit takes over. As years of project work progress, former students and teachers have paved leadership roles, which makes it easier to add, develop, and strengthen contributions and leadership roles in specific topic areas—one step at a time—in our own schools and communities, at our own rate, with the support of others nationwide doing the same.

Simple models that invite engagement are essential for a K-12 national model; they are essential for the experiential learning and outcomes our children are so eager to find in their schools, in their relationships with teachers and communities, and in the real world.

## National and Community Checklists

A national checklist populated with many projects serves as a resource for work in our communities. As we prioritize and select projects of value, an individualized community checklist forms, which shows us who is managing a topic or project, what is needed, and how we are progressing.

If students or community members feel that a particular project from the national checklist is a priority, it can go onto the community checklist. If a community-based organization identifies a particular project of value, it can also go on the community checklist to bring it to the attention of community members. The community checklist coordinates local community information, reduces duplication of effort, and displays needs that may not be common knowledge among all community members. The community checklist shows where the gaps are in meeting local community needs and how community members can contribute.

The extraction of projects for our youth—beginning with kindergartners—is an organizational prioritization to ensure an educational foundation for our citizenry. Beyond signature projects identified with early-grade curriculum and leadership roles, other projects become available to the community, including those in middle school and high school.

# Incorporating New Information and Projects

With a K-12 service learning model in place, all community members come to know that our youth are actively engaged in keeping all local community service work intact and that our youth are connected nationwide and reaching out globally. The most expedient way to disseminate new information to the community is through this educational channel.

One current example of how students and schools can alert community members about new information is in the recycling of plastic bottle caps. For years, people were told they could not be recycled and became accustomed to simply throwing them out, but the recycling industry can now incorporate these caps into the recycling stream. The shift to get everyone onboard to recycle these bottle caps requires communication and education. Students can inform community members that, as small as these bottle caps are, over a billion pounds of them are produced every year, and the recovery of this material is of value in recycled products.

In this particular example, recycling equipment and capabilities need to be checked at the local level. Sixth graders in the leadership role for recycling could take the next steps. A phone call or e-mail to a waste management facility would garner community-specific information. Information in hand, they could create a presentation for a school assembly, coordinating with others in their school district and nationwide as they watch for shifts in statistical data due to these new processes.

With six years of cumulative leadership experience and guidance from teachers, new information and processes provide a natural, progressive opportunity for sixth graders to exercise communication skills and confirm their roles in addressing real-world issues. Classes with leadership roles stay in touch with their community partner organizations, update their checklist topics with new information, and contact news media to disseminate information to the larger community.

## ONE CENTRAL OFFICE

One of the beautiful aspects of service work is that there is rarely a sense of competition. An atmosphere of cooperation and the desire to seek the best outcomes and share information is the norm. When these qualities are modeled from the top down as well as from the bottom up, it's possible to achieve an outcome compatible with the content, a homogenous whole.

The best information comes from the trenches. Perspective from those working hands-on must be the controlling element for all aspects of the design and structure of the initiative. We need grassroots directive and the help of the many who, set to work, will generate the most feedback in the shortest time. Despite variations, commonalities that guide and define projects will emerge.

We need support from the top, as well—at the national level—to facilitate this initiative. A national support point provides a way to organize ourselves—a way for all of us to get on the same page and start together on similar projects. Support at the top gives us a single location for needed resources, one funnel point for all suggestions on existing projects, and submission of new projects. In this initiative, the top could provide structure and funding incentives.

One central office could create and maintain a website with national and global project models. Staff there could work with project originators on replication models and manage input from project replicators. The office would communicate with other developed nations participating in the K-12 service initiative and network with offices that coordinate sister-city relationships.

One central office would provide a cohesive structure for the flow of information to and from ourselves as "the people" joined in a common endeavor. The office would facilitate the work "of the people" by mirroring the qualities of the work itself: sharing information and seeking best outcomes in an atmosphere of cooperation.

# Funding

Many service learning projects do not require external funding. Community members often willingly donate supplies, and beginning grade school projects involve minimal if any expense. Existing systems of support with matching mission values, such as AmeriCorps and SeniorCorps, would be a natural fit with a K-12 service learning curriculum.

While voluntary community participation and support for the initiative has its merits, federal funding is appropriate, as service learning outcomes directly address many relevant issues brought to the federal level for support and solution. Participation in K-6 projects, substantiated by documented outcomes from partnering community-based organizations, could be rewarded with federal funding for more-involved, higher-level service learning projects on the national checklist.

As with any grassroots initiative, people and inspiration are the fuel. We continue to learn from projects in developing areas of the world that ownership among community members is critical. Readily accessible projects with specific tasks allow community members to identify a contribution they can make that fits with their lives, budgets, or areas of expertise.

As the initiative starts, support will come from our families, schools, service organizations, churches, and businesses. We have the manpower among ourselves, and we have the supply; we simply need to organize and distribute.

Some communities can afford materials for an elementary grade project while others may not. Some projects will take off quickly and easily, while others will grow slowly. Some projects may not meet local needs, while others may generate excess. If a project is up and running well in our community, the decision can be made to reach out and give our excess to a location where others are struggling to meet a severe need.

As our children come together nationally to share statistics, they will see distribution of wealth; their altruistic capabilities, still well supported in early grades, will naturally suggest outreach when they have excess; they will want to see the balances readjust. They will clearly see—and the model will help them—that need can be met with excess and that we can reach out not only in our own communities or to a global sister city but to national areas of need, strengthening the fabric of peer relationships nationwide.

Companies willing to donate supplies or funds are additional sources of funding. With all our children working together and submitting their outcomes to a national database, pockets of greatest need will become clearer to all, allowing companies to donate to these areas of greatest need more quickly and efficiently.

## THE LOGIC OF STARTING YOUNG

Long-lasting solutions seem to elude adults, which ultimately disappoints our children. Ironically, those who can help are the youngest, those who have the purest vision. Children adjust the adult lens toward purity of vision for the world.

Without the inclusion of our children, the problem solving we attempt as adults will be flawed. If we are to change direction toward infectious solution-making, we will need humility to see through their lens, believe in the simplicity of their logic, and endorse the significance of their presence. If we work with our youth, listen to them for guidance, and contribute the organizational skills we possess as adults, we can create a legacy of which we can be proud.

Children are capable of more than we allow. They are eager for inclusion in real-life activities, and they constitute a large segment of our population. Because we know that habits are formed early in life, we begin reading to children when they are very young. We can approach the area of service and community involvement in the same way to unlock our children's potential to grow in understanding of problems and solutions and in developing interest in lifelong community service.

Thirteen years of K-12 education is long—especially from the perspective of youth. Test scores and grades are superficial status checks on the growth and well-being of our youth. The framework of their education, defined by previous generations and without the inclusion of their perspective or voice, remains firmly fixed as they grow in awareness of their constantly changing world in which they have as yet no inclusion.

During the last phase of their school experience, a significant number of young Americans drop out. Concern for this phenomenon has caused educators across the country to devise programs to keep these young adults engaged in their final years of schooling, but we are beginning too late in the process to address this issue. Something more fundamental is missing.

A K-12 national service learning model brings contrast and balance to the existing educational framework. If we begin at the beginning, in kindergarten, adding a critical missing ingredient during this highly formative period of growth, the result is altered; as in the presence of a catalyst, outcomes shift.

Perhaps high school dropout issues would fade away under the positive influence of real-life engagements further supported by community programs that mentor our youth. Perhaps students would look forward to the passage of leadership roles in their schools and in their communities. Perhaps they would feel better about school and the opportunity to make a difference. Perhaps their K-12 service journals would become a record of living history—of their personal contributions and value in the world, a meaningful record of their schooling they would keep and even pass on to the next generation. Perhaps they would take pride in accomplishments that surpass the efforts of their elders. Perhaps world tensions would begin to melt as youth follow the lead of project originators to support their peers in developing areas of the world. Perhaps habits of disregard for the environment would shift to truly sustainable processes.

When a service learning project originator spoke to a district-wide gathering of third graders in 2006, he referred to them as the class of 2016. Bringing this vantage point to the awareness of our youth strengthens purpose and identity. It also reminds us, as adults, of who they are, and who they will be.

Americans have been innovative pioneers from the beginning. Instead of continuing to apply the same standard measures of accomplishment that don't capture the inspired interest of our youth, if we were to open the scope of education to involve them in real-life work with us, we might discover powerful gifts they have to bring to our world that exceed our ability to anticipate the outcomes.

## A COMMON HERITAGE OF CIVIC ENGAGEMENT

Our nation, created by its citizens, was founded on freedom and equality. Incorporating an experiential civic education curriculum for our youth that fosters the concept "of the people, by the people, and for the people" exemplifies our foundational concepts. Think "of the average person," "of the specialized expert," "of a child" and a convergence of these as an average person gets a suggestion from an expert and involves children in the process. As we work together, we will create solutions of value in the community, nationally, and worldwide. With the aid of our technology, we can come together with the support of our common humanity focused through the lens of our children. A national point of dissemination would facilitate communication and renew inspiration for a government that works for and with the people, encouraging them to suggest, create, and refine solutions without control measures that might inhibit best outcomes.

As we come together as Americans, we will learn from and be inspired by one another. Those who take the lead will show us the path and reach out with support to bring us onboard. As our children see other children, as teachers see other teachers, as parents see other parents, as principals and superintendents see other administrators accomplishing project objectives, a convergence and flow of collective energy will carry us forward.

We have never come together to see what would happen if we positively embraced one another in sustained community service. Communication and coordination technology is poised to initiate this potential. To envision that this sustained developmental work—drawing on the best ideas in a variety of realms with our children at the helm—could bring widespread peace and productivity is not a quantum leap but an easily attained outcome based on resources at hand.

As we broaden our perspective, we can see the integration of national and global elements that affect our families and local communities. A national model would strengthen our national identity—not only as we perceive ourselves, but also as others around the world perceive us by our actions and commitment. Once up and running, the model easily coordinates with other developed nations, working with them to adopt sister cities in developing areas of the world and coordinating work on environmental issues—sharing the positive results of these efforts worldwide. We would build extensive relations at home and abroad from a sustained base of outreach.

Beginning at the local level is something we can see and understand. Local organizations make us aware of local problems, and a national checklist of projects can provide solutions. Reaching out to others nationally as we meet local needs and have excess would strengthen our national unity. Similar organizations in similar communities are often problem solving similar difficulties. Sharing processes and outcomes promotes efficiency and allows us to see where there are excesses and deficiencies and help one another on a national level.

Helping those in developing areas brings us together in solving issues of environmental concern and peaceable coexistence. As every community works with a sister city, shared problem solving increases significantly. Bringing solutions, often generated by indigenous people, to areas of the world in need can positively impact our world standing. Relationships developed between children worldwide will influence their adult-world relations in the future.

Fast-forward to consider the time when the cycle is repeating for the children of the first round of parents who themselves engaged in K-12 service learning; they will bring a wealth of experience to their children's service learning education, and there will be parents worldwide who were on the receiving end of the service outreach in sister-city relationships. Imagine a world that continually receives intelligent giving and operates from a base of cooperative relationships.

Building a common core of service learning projects managed by our youth reaches down to the roots of our citizenry to create comprehensive, sustained outreach to those in need, a heritage of civic engagement. We can come together with unity of purpose as people with common challenges united in ongoing problem solving. With a base model of service learning projects in all school systems, children and families have a point of commonality with others across the United States, and our heritage of civic engagement becomes a topic of conversation that celebrates our accomplishments and our ability to build meaningful relationships locally, nationally, and globally through the inclusion of our youth.

## MOVING FORWARD

The exceptional must become common; we need to move beyond acknowledgment of outstanding projects and shift to widespread replication of those projects so they become commonplace everywhere. With common models, we can add, refine, and share in the larger celebration of what we are accomplishing in our community, our state, and across the nation.

We could begin with the next class of kindergartners or start with a variety of elementary grade projects. A few school-wide projects such as Food2Share or a program that aims at zero waste provide opportunity for all students to get onboard in their schools and nationwide. Our kids will get this. They will see the beginnings of something they can believe in, something they can invest in and be proud of, something that allows them to contribute and find success beyond the framework of test scores and grades.

As we become more involved in doing, we have less time to argue because interest in ideas that work takes over and we find commonality in that. The evidence of accomplishment strengthens unity. As we create this new initiative and move beyond preexisting definitions, questions or potential obstacles will arise. Beyond the projects, we need to prepare to meet these questions and obstacles to keep our forward momentum.

We need to ask whether any idea strengthens or weakens our ability to move forward: Does it help us achieve better outcomes, or does it hold us back with unnecessary processes and paperwork? Does the idea help us to take action or complicate our ability to do so? We may find that some teachers or schools are initially resistant to participate, but with our highly developed communication systems, students everywhere can reach out and work together to problem solve start-up challenges.

The idea that any of our children should be deprived of the opportunity to give and better their communities will become unconscionable among us. As we truly come together, bringing the best of our giving, our intelligence, our communication systems, and our resources, we will generate a momentum that will carry us forward with strength, gathering more and more of us into the work of creating a better world.

Is it possible for us to agree? Of course. As Americans, we have the entrepreneurial vision to carve a new path. I have yet to encounter a teacher, principal, superintendent, parent, community member, public servant, or staff member of a community-based organization who finds fault with the logic of this initiative. When disasters occur, we mobilize, but we are capable of mobilizing without such prompts. We do this in businesses and in our families—we plan and create solutions, adjusting as we go, incorporating professional advice and considerations.

However our beginnings take off, we will create more than we already have. As we all begin, more models and ways to accomplish objectives will surface and circulate. The actions of project originators and project replicators will energize us. Even the smallest initial outcomes will inspire us. Where needs exist without solutions, American ingenuity will surface. We *can* do this.

## THE QUEST TO REALIZE THE K-12 SERVICE INITIATIVE

As Charlotte's Circle grew and the outcomes became evident, we could see the long-term potential for its replication. I asked our New York service learning coordinator several questions:

- Why do we hear of outstanding projects in other states yet not replicate them in our own?

- Why do these projects remain where they started?
- Why do we read about and comment on these projects but just go about business as usual?
- Why don't we replicate outstanding service projects that are of value in any community on a national level?

Five years ago, there was no answer to these questions, and they remain unanswered. Many organizations across the country identify wonderful problem-solving projects, but they are only narrowly replicated. Service learning projects in our schools take place randomly with sporadic engagement from year to year based on the interest of individual teachers. Autonomy reigns from state to state and district to district. Organizing them at the national level does not fit current systems.

A K-12 service initiative is a large-scale undertaking. Most national service-related organizations are set up to address part of a larger whole and are therefore not able to do much more than confirm the logic or the timeliness of the idea; they are not able to take action that would move a national K-12 concept forward. The magnitude of change is simply beyond their scope, with no common reference point for comparison. Although the initiative is large in scale, embracing national and international dissemination, it is so common-sense oriented that it is readily understood by people from any walk of life. It addresses the inclusion of our children and solving basic life problems that are familiar territory. It is a simple yet comprehensive organizational strategy.

This K-12 initiative—clearly defined and organized, with well-designed structural support and incentives going beyond the purely altruistic—has the capacity to stimulate our latent energy. If we were all informed, if we all got the blueprint, if we all connected through the Internet—not just sharing ideas, but plans, projects, a checklist, a game plan, and outcomes among ourselves—inspiration would run high. Simpler, entry-level projects that don't require federal funding would commence the initiative with ease. As schools and community members sustain these primary foundational projects—with outcomes substantiated by local nonprofits—school districts would then qualify for federal support to engage in next-level projects that may require funding.

At this point in the process, everyone in the community can take pride in their accomplishments and the leadership roles our students are taking to bring this about as they bring exemplary projects to their home communities.

Because the major obstacle is not funding, the idea for the initiative falls into a nonexistent category. It does not need a grant, and it doesn't require a nonprofit to be established to get the initiative off the ground. It needs to be executed from a place or position of power to reach us all. For the K-12 service initiative to take off, structural support is required from the very top.

There is essentially one place for the initiative to begin: the president. The office of the president is familiar with the magnitude of our converging issues and needs. This office embraces the management and ongoing assessment of large-scale undertakings and the overlaps that can exist between initiatives. The logic and timeliness the model would bring to the overall mass of problem solving would be seen from the perspective of this office, and it could identify next steps and connections to move the initiative toward full-scale realization. This office is simply the most appropriate in relation to the idea and its execution.

While I understand the perhaps naivety of such a suggestion, as this office is extremely inundated and insulated, I nonetheless feel this to be not only the best and most efficient route but also the *only route* for this to occur and draw us together nationally and globally. My meetings and conversations with a variety of offices I thought could offer support have brought me to this realization, which has in turn motivated me to paint this picture of the concept and to seek the support of others to bring it to fruition.

We have the technological tools to draw our youth together in this endeavor worldwide; all we need is the organizational structure to connect us all, to share outcomes, and to create a collective wave of change in our communities and in their sister cities.

I left my profession in music to pursue the development of the K-12 service learning model and its national dissemination. I have reached out to a plethora of logical contacts over the past five years, including senators, members of congress, and congressional committees. I've met with staff in the Department of Education, the Corporation for National and Community Service, Learn and Serve, and the Department of Defense. Their consensus is that the initiative is "where we need to be" and "ahead of the curve." I even handed a copy of the outline to the secretary of education but have not yet connected with the right person or office who can bring this to the attention of those with the power to execute this initiative. The difficulty, at present, lies in the singular nature of the objectives that most agencies hold, as they do not have the power to create an overarching design that would create a focused structure.

If this could be brought to the attention of the president, we would get there. The president would see the multiple overlaps of solutions this would bring at home and abroad and could launch the initiative. How inspiring would it be for our kids, our nonprofits, our community members, and all Americans to see the president supporting their contributions to society and recognizing their value? They would see that power is not held by a few and that we are all getting on the same page.

The impact of our children's questions and suggestions as they bring outstanding project models to the awareness of their home communities for replication would be beyond our current frame of reference. As Americans, we generate solutions; we look for next steps; we are interested in progression; we are inventive. Let's engage our children in solving problems that matter and get excited with them and for their involvement in leading us into a new era.

Our children do not represent just hope for the future. Working with us now, they can embrace solutions in the present and confirm our common humanity and the "reach out now" capacity we readily access as Americans when crises occur. Our world standing allows us to inspire others worldwide. We are known for taking action. We see and acknowledge better ways to do things and get excited by outstanding project models with needful solutions. We give of our time, our thought, and other personal resources. We are willing to do what it takes to work for the environment and to help others. The list of our contributions is enormous and continues to grow.

A national K-12 service initiative makes sense to the average citizen, is immediately actionable, embraces existing systems of support, has short- and long-term outcomes, and is sustainable for the long haul worldwide. It identifies outstanding projects, honors project originators, and incorporates ongoing input from teachers, students, and community organizations. It gives people something practical to do in their communities that unities them with others nationally and globally, reviving the American spirit and awakening the true sense of community with our children at the helm. This K-12 initiative will surpass anything we have created thus far, providing a legacy for our children globally, and creating significantly different outcomes than those we presently experience. The model builds an infrastructure of civic engagement at home as well as abroad, rooting the positive outcomes of widespread service activity as the norm. The adults of today are not prepared to address the challenges we face, but our children can become prepared.

With shared values, common areas of problem solving, and uniquely American ingenuity, we can rediscover the heartbeat of our nation and come together to embrace those in need, and, for the first time, include the youngest Americans.

# AN ADDENDUM

▼

What follows is a narrative detailing the way a service project naturally evolved in our community, providing an example of how a service project can take on a momentum that contributes in many unexpected ways. Though not intended as a service learning project, which is most commonly associated with schools, it embraced preparation, action, reflection, and celebration.

Two summers ago, my husband and I dropped Charlotte off at summer camp in Vermont. I stopped in a yarn store and found this:

## Calling All Knitters:

During World War 11 "Knit Your Bit" appeared on a famous poster showing a pair of socks in progress including the line, "Our boys need socks!"

Today our military men and women need helmet liners. Uncle Sam provides only silk liners, and an industrious local group has been knitting helmet liners in washable wool to keep our soldiers warm. When a wool helmet liner has been provided to someone we usually hear back that everyone in their group would like one.

With requests from one to fifty helmet liners at a time, we could sure use your help.

If you know someone in the military who needs one, or if you can help knit for others please contact us.

We knit as a group on Sunday afternoons from 1-5 pm, at Green Mountain Fibers Yarn Shop on Woodstock Ave, Rutland, or you can knit at home and bring in the finished liners. We'll get them to a soldier who's cold.

And if you'd like to sit & knit with us on Sundays and work on your own project that's fine, too. We love company.

The comment that caught my attention was, "When a wool helmet liner has been provided to someone, we usually hear back that everyone in the group would like one." A completed helmet liner was on display at another store, so I took a photo.

On the way home, I thought about knitting a helmet liner, as the owner of the yarn store had given me a copy of the flyer with the knitting instructions. The idea I could make this and bring some measure of comfort and an expression of care to an American soldier in a complex circumstance was compelling, so I decided to make one.

By December I had completed a helmet liner and was very proud of my new creation. My husband tried it on and it fit beautifully. With some inquiry spread through friends we found that Joe, one of our police officers, was part of a National Guard engineering company headed to Afghanistan. I told him about the project, and he agreed to accept my helmet liner on New Year's Day. He was unsure of the item, as he had never seen one, and he seemed shy about the unexpected gift. He agreed to put it on, as I wanted to be sure that it fit. Then I wanted a photo. Mission complete . . . well, almost.

I asked how many soldiers would be with him and when he was leaving; he told me there were 180 soldiers in the company, which was departing mid-February. Until then, I had not entertained the idea of outfitting his company. One step at a time, I had arrived in the same inspirational space as the knitters in Vermont, knowing the soldiers would appreciate these helmet liners.

Over the next few days, as I toyed with the idea of how to make 180 liners, family members came up with ideas. My husband's aunt suggested a radio interview, my husband suggested a newspaper interview, my daughter Genevieve suggested making a version of the Vermont flyer with our information and a completion date to enlist the help of our local knitting store.

Each step seemed plausible, so I made phone calls, and Genevieve created a poster. I also contacted the first lieutenant of the company. His response educated me further:

Sandy,

Thank you for taking care of us. It sounds like a cool project. We will definitely be enduring some cold environments between our US training location this February/March and the mountainous regions of Afghanistan next winter. As a suggestion for your flyer, replace "reservists" with "soldiers" because technically we are National Guard and not Reserves (while we are quite similar to our reservist counterparts, we are primarily state run while they are federal). You are correct in stating that we have soldiers from the various locations you listed. We actually have soldiers from 42 of the 62 counties in NY State. We are slated to leave on 21 Feb, which will also be the date of our departure ceremony.

We also found a pattern for neck coolers that met military specifications. They were used in oppressive heat conditions and required sewing skills. We added this option to the poster, providing opportunity for others who did not knit to contribute.

# KNIT HELMET LINERS NEEDED

**WHEN:** February 14, 2010

**FOR:** NY Army National Guard's
827th Engineer Company

**HOW MANY NEEDED?:** 180

**DROP OFF LOCATION & SUPPLIES:**
Knitting It All Together
175 Main Street
Oneonta, NY 13820-2501
(607) 432-2154

**CONTACT:** Sandy McKane
sandymckane@gmail.com
(607) 437-0586

**PATTERN & SUPPLIES:** If you would like to knit a helmet liner, please contact Sandy McKane for the pattern. The wool yarn needed for the liners can be purchased at Knitting It All Together on Main St. in Oneonta.

Soldiers in the 827th Engineer Company come from 42 of New York's 62 counties, including Otsego, Delaware, and Albany, with men and women from Buffalo, Syracuse, Rochester, Long Island and Staten Island as well. The helmets provided for soldiers have no lining or just a thin silk lining. These wool helmet liners provide much needed and appreciated warmth. When a wool helmet liner is provided to one soldier, requests are forwarded that everyone in their unit or company would like one.

Our goal is to send off these soldiers with a caring gift from home, providing a helmet liner for each member of this company. We have been informed that there will be 180 soldiers who will leave for training on February 15th. They will train in Wisconsin until April, when they will deploy to Afghanistan for approximately one year.

**NOT A KNITTER?** We will also strive to provide a neck cooler for each soldier. If you sew and would like to contribute to this project, please contact Sandy for information and coordination (see below).

**MONETARY DONATIONS:** If you know of someone who would like to contribute to the cost of supplies, please refer them to Sandy at the contact information above.

The knitters who surfaced were varied. Ella, who was turning eighty-nine, stopped by my house a few times for assistance as she hadn't knitted for some time. Her daughters were exceptionally appreciative of the constructive activity and community involvement the project added to Ella's life. There were women who knitted in the evening after work. Sons requested patterns by e-mail for their mothers who did not have Internet access. Some shared the project with family members in other states. A few women from a nursing home and Girl Scouts ages eight to eleven joined in. Charlotte, who had just learned to knit, completed her helmet liner with a bit of help.

Responses from knitters were inspired:

> You'll be pleased to know that yesterday evening I was working on a helmet liner while commuting home on the train. I had noticed when some "tourists" got on the train and had given them my seat so all four could sit together, and I just scooted across the aisle to where a seat was vacant. After a while, the grandma in the group asked me what I was knitting. So I told her about the project, and she got excited because she is a knitter and belongs to two groups in Maryland. Since I had just been searching the web page for the neck cooler pattern, I had the web address memorized, so gave her that link to look up the helmet liner pattern. Then we exchanged e-mails so I could send her the neck cooler information when I received it from you.
>
> I've just ordered 20 more skeins of yarn to keep working on the helmet liners. I assume the charcoal and mocha colors were okay? I really like the superwash yarn, and it is so soft.
>
> I continue to knit the liners and will gladly send them to you if you need more. I have yarn for about 12-14, and if there is a need, I'll get more yarn. I had to wait over an hour at my husband's doctor's office, so I sat and knitted. I find that the knitting project is very transportable, so I bring it along just in case I have to wait for whatever.

Over 100 knitters and sewers joined the effort. Similar to service learning projects, information flowed among those involved to create best outcomes. I received ten beautiful knitted helmet liners from a woman who had been making them in batches of ten over the past three years. She shared an alternative yarn to the one suggested in the pattern. It met the criteria of 100 percent wool at about half the cost. She was also able to suggest the exact colors in this brand of yarn. I then e-mailed our yarn stores involved with the project:

> Considering the ongoing cost of yarn for the knitters (more important to some than others), what do you think of considering

this yarn for the project? Is it something that you could order? Here's my reason for asking:

One of the interesting, community-building aspects of this project is that it is supporting small businesses—yarn stores. The knitters are coming to you for yarn, for help, and as a drop-off point. I think this is a valid aspect of the project that should be preserved. I have a rather large distribution list to communicate with all the knitters who have engaged in this project. Before I write to all our knitters, I want to know what your perspective is on this alternative yarn, as I could let them know about this yarn and if you can stock it.

All the store owners were happy to comply and joined in the spirit of the project by quickly obtaining the yarn.

Another woman whose husband had served in the military contacted me. Her husband was allergic to wool, so she suggested alpaca as an alternative. Although the yarn was considerably more expensive, a few were made.

As the February 15 deadline approached, packages started to arrive. Our stores had boxes full of completed helmet liners we picked up. One store had been hanging them up:

One of the store owners shared this perspective:

> I think it's wonderful how the community of knitters has embraced this project. It is especially heartwarming to see the looks on their faces when they bring the completed liners in! They are so pleased to be contributing.

Inspiration ran high. Charlotte and a few friends helped sort them into containers for the trip to the National Guard departure ceremony. They were excited to report that although they needed just 180, we had 300.

At the ceremony I described the project to the soldiers and how the knitters had come together to create the liners by their departure date. The neck coolers were also described, noting that labels with instructions were on each item. We showed additional care for their comfort when I asked if any soldiers were allergic to wool; two raised their hands, so they got alpaca liners.

The soldiers lined up to select helmet liners, which varied in color and size. They joked among themselves as they assessed their head sizes in relation to the slight variations in the handmade helmet liners. The company had already packed their gear for transport, but they still had backpacks with pockets that easily accommodated the liners and neck coolers. Their individual comments were very appreciative and respectful of our concern for their well-being. Toward the end of the line, a young female soldier asked if we had any more of the alpaca liners left, and one remained. She explained she had not wanted to openly share a need for this accommodation among her mostly male peers.

That evening I received the following e-mail entitled "Thank You!!!!":

> Hi Sandy,
>
> I just wanted to send you a note of thanks for the wonderful wool liners the upstate NY knitters made for my husband and his fellow soldiers!
>
> Knowing that your group of incredibly kind, caring, and dedicated knitters were working this whole time on these terrific helmet liners is such a great feeling. I now really feel like members of our community have been paying attention, and it is terrific that they all care enough to spend the time to make these liners. It really means a lot to the soldiers and their families.
>
> As family members, all we want is for our soldiers to stay safe and comfortable. I am relieved to know that the liner my husband has will help him stay comfortable throughout this deployment. I must also share with you that the soldiers are quite impressed that the liners were made to army specifications, as that is quite a task!
>
> Thank you so, so much! Please feel free to forward this on to your knitters—they are truly spectacular individuals who have made a significant difference.
>
> Many thanks,
> Erica

My experience with the military is very limited. I did not grow up with family who served, so this communication helped to educate me. My education continued when I was contacted by the mother of a marine who had recently deployed. She had seen a news article about the project.

Dear Sandy,

I had never heard of anyone making or sending helmet liners before. It was so great to hear about this and very generous of the knitters to be doing this to support our soldiers. I do not knit, but I would be willing to help with shipping expenses if you could send some of these liners to my son, age 21, and his platoon. I think they would really appreciate the thoughtfulness and the comfort that the liners would give them. I am sure you have received many requests, but I thought it wouldn't hurt to inquire.

Thank you for your consideration.
Cheryl

When I asked how many were needed, Cheryl was quick to respond that she would inquire. Through our communications I learned about the distinction between a battalion, a company, and a platoon, and I also got information to share with other knitters:

We have been told not to repeat anything that might make their location, maneuvers or company known; anything to do with the size of the battalion or where they are stationed.

My son said it is cold now in Afghanistan so the liners will be greatly appreciated. They will be very surprised, I'm sure, and it means a lot to us as parents to be able to send them the liners. Our contact from his camp said to please pass on a big "thank you" from her as well as the company commander. They really appreciate things like this and said they have heard about the liners and have had very positive remarks from the troops receiving them.

When I asked Cheryl about a possible interview, her response revealed a more sensitive family perspective on military service:

This is a very hard time for us; having a child in the military and then having to send them off to a foreign country, the unknown.

It is a time for us just to reflect on our family as we watch and wait. I appreciate all you are doing and hope you understand.

We continued to collect valuable project information as Cheryl worked on shipping:

Space available mail is less expensive; packages ship only as space is available in bins upon departure and need to weigh under 15 lbs. Small boxes are shipped more quickly as they fit in remaining small spaces. The total cost to send 140 helmet liners was $21.

Cheryl had offered to pay for shipping and sent the address for me to ship the liners to Afghanistan. I suggested that she should have more direct involvement in the process, as she had remarked, "it means a lot to us as parents to be able to send them the liners." I also knew how inspiring it was to handle so many hand-made items—such an outpouring of giving. She agreed to come get them.

Two days after she picked them up from my home, she sent the following e-mail. I asked her if I could forward it to all the knitters and she responded: "Please feel free to send it on. I think they should know how much this means to those receiving the helmet liners and the families at home."

Good evening Sandy,

I got two identical boxes at work yesterday. Seventy fit nicely in the first box, with the remaining in the second box. As I repacked the helmet liners into these two boxes, I couldn't help but read the tags to see who had generously knitted them. I read names from all over the area. One tag said (I wish I had written it down but to the best of my memory) "I am a pacifist but support you and pray for your safety."

Wow . . . deep breath. You were so right about handling the helmet liners, seeing all the different knitters names, seeing the helmet liners' instructions . . . the handwritten instruction tags . . . the message above. I am overwhelmed. These 100 or more knitters should feel a great deal of pride for accomplishing this. This means so much to the families at home as well as the family member receiving these. Thank you for bringing all these knitters together. Thanks to all the knitters for the time, money, love, and compassion they put into their work. I felt it all as I held each one and repacked them into the boxes. If you ever wondered if there was enough room in this world to make a difference, I can personally tell you *yes*. Yes, you can make a world of difference and you have.

Thank you from the bottom of my heart.
Cheryl

A few weeks later, Cheryl sent a response from the chaplain who had distributed the helmet liners among the marines:

The helmet liners disappeared in about 15 minutes—all of them. As it is already warming up here, that came as a bit of a surprise.

The knitters in Vermont were pleased to learn of the project's ripple effect in New York:

Thank you for the pictures, and thank you so much for taking the initiative to coordinate your own effort for your area. All done within a month or a bit more! I am forwarding this information to my fellow knitters so they will learn how their involvement in this project for our troops catalyzed others to use their skills to help and honor our soldiers.

Over the summer, I continued to reach out to a variety of military offices to find another company, as many knitters continued to make helmet liners. When I went to the website we used for patterns, the project was no longer listed, as the military was going to begin supplying helmet liners made of a wicking material. While this was good news, as all service personnel would benefit, the additional option of the handmade item would promote community awareness and support for those serving in the military.

This service project can be framed to identify service learning:

## Preparation

Identifying all the preliminary steps to inform and organize, incorporating information and perspective from family members, knitters, soldiers, and others.

## Action

Making contacts, interviews, creating flyers, distributing patterns, maintaining communications, knitting the liners, sewing the neck coolers, and collecting and distributing the liners.

## Reflection

So many moments for reflection occur as information and perspective from within the realm of the military surfaces and responses come from a variety of community members and knitters from different generations.

## Celebration

Giving the helmet liners to the soldiers at their departure ceremony, sharing the photos of all the helmet liners collected, the National Guard ceremony description, and responses from military family members with all the knitters.

In a national checklist of projects, if helmet liners were still a genuine need, the project could go under national needs/military with other project topics:

Deployed Soldiers:

- Care packages
- Cell phones/phone cards
- Books
- Letter-writing
- Help for families

Veterans:

- Honor
- Recovery
- Disability
- Employment
- Housing

With a checklist of national and global service projects and a base of service learning in our schools, we would also come to know of the value of knitting programs in schools, programs that occur during recess and after school. We could turn to Seth Boyden Elementary School in New Jersey for model components to start a program for knitting in elementary school, discovering the community-building outcomes they have found that affect the overall school environment. In the global checklist, we would find examples of knitters coming together for employment and also as an activity that promotes healing in the aftermath of intense conflict. The implications in both realms point to the commonality of knitting as a calming, constructive, community-building activity that promotes intergenerational relationships.

Joe, the original National Guard Soldier, returned to our home community in his professional role as a city police officer. I see him from time to time—in uniform or as a civilian. When we make eye contact, I always feel a moment of recognition—of a caring connection that he and I will always share. Without my service involvement, this perception would not exist. This is the type of moment in my life when I feel value in my presence on earth.

# ABOUT THE AUTHOR

▼

The seeds for the idea of a national K-12 service initiative were planted in 2000, when author Sandy McKane's then five-year-old daughter started wrapping coins with her grandfather, and then donated that money to a local charity. As time went on, her daughter, Charlotte, expanded her giving, gained supporters, and in 2003 started tracking donations, which totaled $1,457 for the year. By the following year, donations had risen to $5,864, and New York State Senator Seward had presented McKane's daughter with a commendation from the New York State Senate.

Inspired by the progression of learning that she was witnessing in her daughter at such a young age, McKane began exploring service learning possibilities beyond the scope of her daughter's contributions. She developed a first year seminar—The Human Spirit in Action: Service Learning—at Hartwick College in upstate New York, where she was chair of the music department. Over several years, the students in her seminar developed and implemented a program called Food2Share—an ongoing, self-sustaining system to address food insecurity in local communities.

McKane went on to establish the Oneonta Service Learning Project, creating workshops for local elementary teachers to develop service learning projects for their students. She also presented at a number of service learning conferences, covering topics that addressed gathering projects from national resources and developing service learning projects for very young children.

In 2004, McKane was the recipient of a Learn & Serve mini-grant to support the development of early-grade service learning projects. In 2005 she received a Special Legislative Education Grant from Senator Seward's office to further the development of the Oneonta Service Learning Project. In 2006 the author left her position as chair of the music department and dedicated herself to developing the framework for a K-12 service initiative that could be rolled-out nationwide. This book is the culmination of her work toward that end.

Sandy lives in upstate New York with her husband Tim, and their two dogs, Isabella and Oscar. When not working on the service initiative or at the piano, Sandy can be found in her garden, knitting, making jewelry, or taking weekend trips into Manhattan to visit her older daughter, Genevieve.